Contemporary architectural
Images

Whitney

Author Francisco Asensio Cerver

Editorial Manager Jordi Vigué

Project Coordinator Iván Bercedo

Graphic Design Mireia Casanovas Soley

Layouts Òscar Lleonart Ruiz
Jaume Martínez Coscojuela
Cristina Suñé González

Translation David Buss
Proofreading Elaine Fradley
Copy-editing Viviane Vives

Published by

Whitney Library of Design

An imprint of Watson & Guptill Publications

New York

© 1998 Francisco Asensio Cerver

ISBN: 0-8230-0932-7

Printed in Spain

Gràfiques Ibèria s.a.

Beyond the gravitational effect which maintains bodies in orbit, all sentient atoms are lost in space. Each atom pursues its own path towards infinity and loses itself in space. This is exactly what we are seeing in our current society, which seems to be hell-bent on accelerating all moving bodies, all messages, in fact, all processes of all types; this, together with today's mass communication media, has created for each event, story, or image a simulated path towards infinity. Each historical, political, or cultural fact is loaded with a kinetic energy that wrenches it from its own space and propels it into a hyperspace where all meaning is lost, given that it can never return from there.

[Jean Baudrillard, L'illusion de la fin ou la grève des événements. Editions Galilée. Paris, 1992.]

Anyone who has ever tried it knows that photographing a building can be a difficult and very unrewarding job. How can one photograph a four hundred and fifty foot skyscraper, or an airport with a nine hundred foot façade, not to mention a building sited in a very narrow street, or a nine foot square bath? While the human eye can make a quick sweep of what it sees, enabling the brain to compose an overall picture, the camera cannot work in the same way. It remains a fixed mechanism only able to establish an actual point of view, or angle of vision. The nearer the camera is to the object, the more difficult it is to include everything in the composition. In a narrow street, for example, it is practically impossible to obtain a complete, flat image of a façade. Similarly, it is practically impossible to get an overall view of a domestic interior. Even using a very wide-angle lens, the edges of the image are deformed and leak away. The leaking can be corrected by the use of bellows but not the deformations; consequently, the more comprehensive the photo of an interior, the less real is the size correlation between the objects on the edge and those in the center of the photo. We only have to look at photos displaying round pillars to see them converted into ellipses. Likewise, if two objects are distant from each other, it is impossible to maintain both of them in focus, but if the viewpoint is only partial, it is impossible to get an overall image of the space.

These dilemmas seem almost banal when compared with the difficulties encountered in capturing the light and color of objects, as light and, in consequence, the tone of the materials, change constantly. Excessive sunlight, a shadow, or a reflection from a nearby building can change a photo completely. Indoors, the contrast between the weak interior light and the intense natural light of the exterior can make the windows seem to be burning or the rooms too dark. Reflections, artificial lighting, or even the type of film used can give an unreal tone to the photo. If we add to all this the possible distortions that can occur in the process of transferring the photo from the camera to the printed page—developing, scanning, duplicating, printing—it is not surprising that a green wall becomes blue, a red one brown, or a white one yellow.

Some excellent designs are very difficult to photograph, while excellent photographs can be taken of not-so-good projects. Another factor is that the photographer's vision may count for more than the object captured, as evidenced by Klein's photos of New York or Brassai's vision of Paris. The images we see become valuable elements in their own right, surpassing a purely documental role.

Given all these factors, it is not difficult to see that the idea that photos of buildings depend on the buildings themselves, and that they are merely accessories after the fact is false. The photographer participates in the architectural debate using a different language and different weapons to the designer. The fact that his work refers to a specific building does not mean that it depends exclusively on it. However, in spite of all this, photography is the main vehicle for the dissemination of architectural knowledge.

Although it could be thought that architecture is a special case—obviously the interior of a private house can not be visited freely as if it were a museum or art gallery—, in fact, in all disciplines, the desire to appreciate a work of art in its actual context is waning. This tendency is due in large part to the fact that a process of decontextualization is indispensable for the work to be converted into a sign; only when this has been achieved can the work be reproduced, exchanged, sold, published, deconstructed and reinterpreted without having to wonder if these processes destroy the work. As a sign, the work is converted into a irreducible object with the durable simplicity of a coin.

In our society, the norm is that works of art, such as paintings, are known through printed reproductions, and such basic questions as the size of the canvas and the treatment of the surface disappear completely. For some artists, such as Rothko, direct perception of the work is indispensable, as the impact depends on an appreciation of how the space where they are located is affected and how they affect the spiritual mood of the spectator. Obviously, even the most expensive art book cannot convey these sensations.

In fact, even in museums and galleries, this process of decontextualization is furthered by placing works of authors who have nothing in common next to each other, with no other information than a title. Thus, in one room dedicated to the art of the sixties, we may see a piece by Donald Judd juxtaposed to a Warhol silk-screen. It is almost impossible to understand a work of art if one does not know the overall trajectory of the author; in addition, if the work is mixed with some other, completely different, confusion reigns supreme. It is not surprising that many people who visit, say, a museum of contemporary art without any knowledge of the artists or their work, come out with the idea, at best, that what they have seen is a series of caprices and at worst, that somebody is pulling their leg.

In theatre, where perceiving the work in situ is unavoidable, the interpretation and vision of the director is valued above the text itself. There is always some revision of the original text, as if nobody wanted to be faithful to it, due to a horror of being thought unoriginal. Just consider Shakespeare; it is rare to see a version of any of his plays in which either the century or the location has not been changed.

This process of detachment from the original object occurs even in literature. Although it may seem almost impossible to refer to a novel without referring to the actual book itself, many people freely give their opinions about an author without having read any of his work, basing their opinions on those of the critics, a television interview, or a magazine article. The interviewer or journalist covering a press conference to launch a new novel usually knows little more than what is contained in the press handout; how ironical then, that what he later writes is probably seen by a much larger number of people than the original book.

All these examples go to show how a type of vacuum is created around the work itself. It is becoming more difficult to have direct knowledge of a body of work, and even if we are lucky enough to have the work standing before us, we discover that all the information we need to attain an exact and enriched understanding has been systematically eliminated.

The majority of architectural journals present designs in isolation, by means of a photographic report accompanied by plans and a short text. The connection between works presented in one issue of a journal is frequently tenuous; for example, it may consist of the most important buildings inaugurated in May, an auditorium in Berlin, a museum in the country, a factory in Basle, and a house in Tokyo. The most to be hoped for is a monographic issue on one architect or one subject–museums, sports halls, houses–, but even then, there is rarely much information about the surrounding buildings or the city where the building is located. Photographers go to great lengths to ensure that a shot of an auditorium does not show the adjacent ugly block of apartments, and that a delightful house is shown with no reference to the freeway that roars by, a few yards away.

A brief glance at the magazine racks confirms that the number of magazines devoted to architecture has risen considerably in recent years. An important design such as the remodeling of the Potsdamer Platz in Berlin, the Guggenheim Museum in Bilbao, or the new Hong Kong airport may appear in a hundred magazines, be photographed from every angle, and contemplated from the most varied and surprising points of view. It is not even necessary that the project be a large one, requiring substantial investment, and implying a significant change in the urban environment. A simple detached house can also be the subject of exhaustive analysis, especially if it is designed by the likes of Rem Koolhaas or Frank Gehry. Even more attention is paid to the classic designs of modern architecture, such as Le Corbusier's Villa Savoye, Frank Lloyd Wright's Waterfall House, Mies van der Rohe's Farnsworth House, or Aalto's Villa Mairea, which are a staple of all architectural journals. These designs are, of course, known by all architects and by most of those with any interest in architecture, but few people have actually visited them, and only a select few have lived or even slept in them.

The only way of really knowing architecture is by inhabiting it. However, this intimate knowledge is generally restricted to a few buildings–our own house and those of family and friends, our workplace, and perhaps the shopping and cultural centers we frequent. We would be very lucky if more than one or two of these buildings had any architectural significance. Thus, the buildings we really know usually lack architectural interest, while those that are interesting are probably only known through magazines, books, exhibitions, conferences or, in the best of cases, through a rapid, organized tourist trip. As Baudrillard accurately recognizes, modern-day culture is usually presented in a completely decontex-tualised way, like "sentient atoms lost in space".

Knowing a building through books or magazines means trusting the photographer and the critic, and what is more, seeing the design at the same time as we see the inter-pretations and reflections to which it is subject. Both the photography and the criti-cism are autonomous activities and businesses leading to a separate product which might be defined as "published architecture". If we finally manage to visit work that we have seen hundreds of times in print, we are more likely to be surprised than to have a feeling of *déjà vu*.

When visiting the Villa Savoye, probably the most studied and written about house of the twentieth century, for the first time, the immediate impression may be that the media image and the real thing are very different. The ramp is much narrower than it seems in photos, the finishes are less purist, there is a skylight over the bath which is never shown, the site is much smaller than we have imagined, and Le Corbusier used color to a much greater extent than is usually said. These details only go to prove that not only the critic's words but also the actual graphic representation of architecture have their own laws which make it impossible to appreciate certain elements of a building while others are being highlighted.

In principle, the solution to these inaccuracies would be to demand objective texts and photos. The text should be a narrative of the conditions faced by the architect, the design and construction process, and a description of the final building. The photos should be a continuous sequence from the most general view to the most detailed, by day and night, in rain and sunshine.

The process of simplification can easily lead to the labeling of movements and fash-ions. As everybody knows, it is enough for a new name to appear and to become iden-tified with a new style, to lead to a series of prototypical works which eventually become consolidated in a style, whether it be high-tech, deconstructionism, minimal-ism, critical regionalism, or post-modernism. What, at first, is nothing more than the personal search of one architect, by means of media diffusion and the appearance of imitators, metamorphoses into a catalogue of clichés. The dynamic of simplification and imitation results in the generation of ever-poorer designs which are more cliched, more startling, and easier to reproduce.

The second half of the twentieth century has seen first sliding windows, and later rough walls of bare concrete, followed by the most classical of pediments, wedged corners, and empty interiors of a blinding whiteness. The influence of the architectural media over the practitioners of architecture is perhaps best seen in those badly designed buildings which seek to disguise their lack of quality by a slavish adherence to fashion and the current idea reigning at a particular moment. The idea of the new has been used to justify the con-struction of idiotic buildings based on the most hilarious ideas. If books detailing the history of architecture collect together the "brightest and best" of each theoretical movement, a walk through the streets of our cities shows the other side of the coin—the worst of each style.

Obviously, good architecture has nothing to do with the use of stylistic clichés, which are soon out of fashion; equally, theoretical reflection is much more than the mere assignation of labels. However, both are adulterated by the inertia of the media in their thirst for immediacy. The problem is not that the media is superficial or sensationalist—there are many serious publications—but rather that the very nature of the medium, paper; the vehicles of expression, text and photos; and the format the works are presented in, which must be adjusted to the magazine's graphic design, all demand an enormous simplification of the material. The only solution to this situation is to recognize the difference between reality and what is published, and to treat books and magazines not as testimonials, but as exercises in reflection.

In a wider sense, questions such as our relationship with the Earth we inhabit, the growth of our cities, or the evolution of constructive techniques cannot be limited solely to the architectural perspective. The participation of philosophers, sociologists, ecologists, and even politicians in these ongoing debates provides a wider range of perspectives. This is helpful in ensuring that architectural publications can reach a level of maturity which involves not only reproducing buildings but incorporating wider and less specific themes into the architectural debate.

The heart of the city

In Toronto, the center is occupied by the Holy Trinity Church, a nineteenth century building much lower than the office blocks which surround it; while in Jakarta, the Dharmala Group tower tries, with its height, to become a reference point for the dispersed city around it.

1. *Holy Trinity Square Toronto, 1986 Moorhead Associates*

2. *Dharmala Group Offices Jakarta, 1988 Paul Rudolph*

3. *View of the Champs Élysées in Paris.*

When architects still thought they could change the way the world looked and transform people's lives, their starting point was the design of homogenous cities, based on the repetition of various types of dwelling units. However, these infinite cities, with their identical landscapes, soon became untenable. The architects specified the ideal height of their cleanly designed buildings, took great pains over the lighting and ventilation of the dwellings, worked with engineers to provide meticulous road systems designed to avoid traffic jams, and, in many cases, remembered to include large areas of open space with sports clubs, swimming pools, and tennis clubs. In spite of all this effort, it was not long before the realization came that these utopian new cities lacked something—a center, a heart, a place of reference for all the citizens of all the neighborhoods. In the homogeneous city it was only possible to wander amongst identical places. All the planned lighting and ventilation did not obviate the need for a center to house institutional, religious, cultural, and leisure buildings— in short, to become the symbolic image of the city.

From the earliest times, true urban life had been thus constructed. The Romans organized their camps—and later their cities—around two perpendicular streets, the Cardus and the Decumanus, whose intersection housed the Forum and the Temple.

During the Renaissance, the importance of the center was so great that the whole city was organized around it. The beaux-arts tradition of axes and grand perspectives was based on the secure knowledge that the great avenues, boulevards, and paths would connect buildings that were monumental and representative.

Thus, when the generation of modern architects commissioned with the reconstruction of the majority of European cities after the Second World War began to confront this challenge, the almost monographic topic of their conferences and discussions was: The Heart of the City: Towards a Humanization of Urban Life.

The most accurate definition of "urbe and polis" is, ironically, similar to that of a cannon: take a hole, surround it with densely packed wire, and the result is a cannon. Thus, the urbe or polis begins as a space: the forum or the agora; everything else is just a pretext to support this space and delimit its contours. The polis is not just a collection of dwelling units, but a meeting point for the citizens, a space devoted to public functions. The urbe is not constructed like a cabin or domus to shelter from the storm and protect the species, which are after all private tasks for each family, but for discussion of civic matters. This means nothing less than the invention of a new type of space, much more

3

The concept of the center varies in different cultures. In Japan, the center is empty. In Tokyo it is occupied by the inaccessible palace of the Emperor. The photo on the opposite page shows an indoor plaza in a financial complex on the outskirts of Tokyo. Executives relax around the artificial pond during their break periods.

4. *Solid Square*
Kanagawa, 1995
Nikken Sekkei

innovative than the space of Einstein.

[From the introductory text to the papers given at the VIII CIAM Congress (Hoddesdon, England, 1951) by Josep Lluís Sert and Ernesto Nathan Rogers.]

Thus, after the catastrophe of the war, modern architects began to concern themselves more with the construction of the civic space than with the definition of a new language for architecture or the formalization of new types of dwelling. Although this interest in studying the city in its totality, integrating architecture and urbanism, dated at least from the publication of the Athens Charter in 1933, it was not until the post-War period that the fundamental concern of architects became not the buildings themselves, but rather the empty space, open public places where people could meet. It is not a coincidence that in the poster for the

VIII CIAM Congress no building is depicted, only a group of people.

During these years, the historical centers of our cities recovered some of their lost prestige and became again the nucleus of civil life. The idea of recentralization took hold, in opposition to the tendency of modern architecture to site itself on the periphery, marginalizing the traditional city. The unavoidable reconstruction of many historical city centers forced modern architects to look again at sites they had previously rejected as being full of obsolete and decadent buildings.

After an era of absolutism, and the unhappiness this caused, it was necessary to reinvent democracy and to think again about the city as it was originally conceived in classical Greece. This is clearly shown by Sert and Rogers' definition of the city in their introduction to the Congress: "The urbe began as a space and everything else is just a pretext to support this space." We are accustomed to regarding the city as a huge agglomeration of buildings, as dense spaces within a wider territory, but for Sert and Rogers, the opposite is true. The city is not just a concentration of people, services, or activities but rather the space that opens up in the middle of this concentration, the void in the density.

A city without squares in which to sit at a sunny café terrace and talk, without boulevards where we can stop and watch the street musicians and mime artists, is not a city. The *polis* is defined by its civic space. This is obviously a partial vision, and one that raises many questions. It tends to identify the public space as a square, a park, or an avenue, when in actuality, in some cities—such as Fez—said space is a ribbon extending from one shop to another, throughout the whole city; while in others, it may be on the sixteenth floor of a skyscraper, or in the dining room of a restaurant. It is clear that what Sert and Rogers were attempting in 1947 was not to define the city but rather to propose a model and, above all, to encourage architects to construct public spaces and define social centers.

The second generation of modern architects—Bakema, the Smithsons, van Eyck, Candilis, etc.—were imbued with the positivist spirit flourishing during the reconstruction of Europe, which sought, above all, the creation of public space for daily life. One example of this spirit is the series of photographs taken by Nigel Henderson of life in London's East

End; displayed by the Smithsons at the last CIAM Congress in Aix-en-Provence in 1953, they played an important part in the gestation of this new architectural sensitivity. When confronted by a landscape in ruins, it did not seem so important to establish a strict order; on the contrary, it was acknowledged that any new actuation should accept, and indeed promote, a certain degree of chance, even anarchy. The photo-collages of the Smithsons seem to be saying that people should be allowed to act freely and that the buildings should be built around their experiences. However, the end result of these reflections is not the traditional city but, rather, proposals for the construction of enormous buildings, acting as whole cities; megastructures extending over the land and forming immense grids.

In effect, the public space has been a constant theme in architecture during the second half of this century. In addition to the CIAM, the subject is reflected in the proposals of the Japanese Structuralists and Metabolists, in the utopian, recreational proposals of the Situationists, in the vindication of the traditional city by Aldo Rossi, in the revisionist theses of postmodernists such as Rob Krier, and in Rem Koolhaas's enthusiasm for the metropolitan. However, in spite of these theoretical efforts, a large part of the cities and neighborhoods actually built during this time are more like a cancerous growth extending over the land than an exemplary *polis* of democratic and harmonious life.

Even in the two most emblematic cases where modern architects have created a whole new prototype city out of nothing, Brasilia and Chandigarh, one cannot find a civic nucleus with activities comparable to those of a traditional city square. Although Le Corbusier, Niemeyer, and Costa did design spaces surrounded by the main public buildings which were meant to serve in this way, in both cases errors of scale turned these squares into monumental or symbolic spaces unfit for the daily activities of the inhabitants.

The urban heritage of this century includes some of the most amorphous and unintegrated spaces ever conceived, such as the neighborhoods of linear, isolated blocks surrounding many of the great European capitals like Milan, Barcelona, and Amsterdam. Another feature of our time is the divided city, with a downtown crowded with skyscrapers, and thousands of acres of low-density suburbs. At the same time, over

4

In historical squares, it is the buildings of the perimeter that give character to the space. In such squares, the challenge is in minimizing the impact of the urban furniture, lighting, and roadways on the image of the square.

5, 6. *Two squares in the centers of Strasbourg and Vitry-sur-Seine*

5

the last thirty years, we have seen the emergence of cities in Asia, Africa, and South America where development has been dominated by the construction of individual buildings. The center of these new cities is found in the lobbies of their tallest buildings, and this is the only law respected.

In summary, if by "the heart of the city" we understand places such as Rockefeller Plaza in New York, Trafalgar Square in London, the Piazza de Spagna in Rome, or Madrid's Plaza Mayor, few places built in the second half of this century can be said to have a similar aspect or function. As the VIII CIAM Congress stated, there is no better heart of the city than its historical center.

In the light of this, if we ask what the future of the city—understood as a space of civic interaction—is, the answers seem to indicate a divided strategy. On one hand, there is the necessity of conserving and recuperating existing historical areas such as civic and social centers, while on the other, there is the need to provide more recently constructed areas with the same amenities.

The majority of European cities have begun the rehabilitation of their historical districts, a process which includes not only the restoration of the most significant buildings and the general renovation of façades but also, in many cases, pedestrianization of important streets and squares. The following pages show some examples of this strategy carried out recently in Lyons, Barcelona, and Strasbourg. In this last city, the urban refurbishment of the city center has been accompanied by an intense campaign in favor of public transport, the city's trams in particular. The danger is that these historical areas could thus be converted into museum pieces. This would result in their loss of dynamism and effectiveness as social centers, an effect clearly counterproductive to what is intended. It should be possible to intervene in the historical city, not only by restoring but also renovating, building, bringing up to date—in short, by imposing a contemporary rhythm on the consolidated texture of the city. This would seem to be the only path to revitalization.

The other side of the coin is reflected in recent projects such as Citizens Plaza in Tokyo and Pershing Square in Los Angeles. In both cases, a great civic space was proposed in a city without a tradition of such spaces; a city where the pedestrian always comes second to the urban freeway, the office block, and the shopping mall. Also common to both projects is the importation of a foreign model, given the lack of an indigenous tradition to fall back on. In Los Angeles, the model was the plaza of the Mexican provincial city, or even the patio of the hacienda, which Ricardo Legorreta has changed in scale and converted into an urban landscape. In Shinjuku, the financial district of Tokyo, the direct reference of Kengo Tange's project is the Italian piazza, such as Saint Peter's in Rome, or the square in Sienna. This strategy echoes that of Arata Isozaki, who revised Michelangelo's town hall square in Rome for the city of Tsukuba.

Adapting a well-known formula to a different environment is not, however, the only option possible. In the quintessential skyscraper city—New York—there is a considerable tradition of civic spaces such as the Rockefeller Center, Times Square, or streets such as 5th Avenue and Madison Avenue. From the construction of the Seagram Building by Mies van der Rohe in Chicago onwards, many builders of skyscrapers have been conscious of the need to include a small square in front of the building, both to integrate it with the city and to give it an otherwise lacking civic dimension. It should be said that this type of space works much better when it is part of an overall plan for the area.

Finally, if we look at the large-scale urban projects being produced at the end of the millennium—such as the remodeling of the Potsdamer Platz in Berlin or the construction of Pudong, the financial district of Shanghai—we can only conclude that this concept of the city center as civic space is currently being treated in a manner that is, to say the least, uneven.

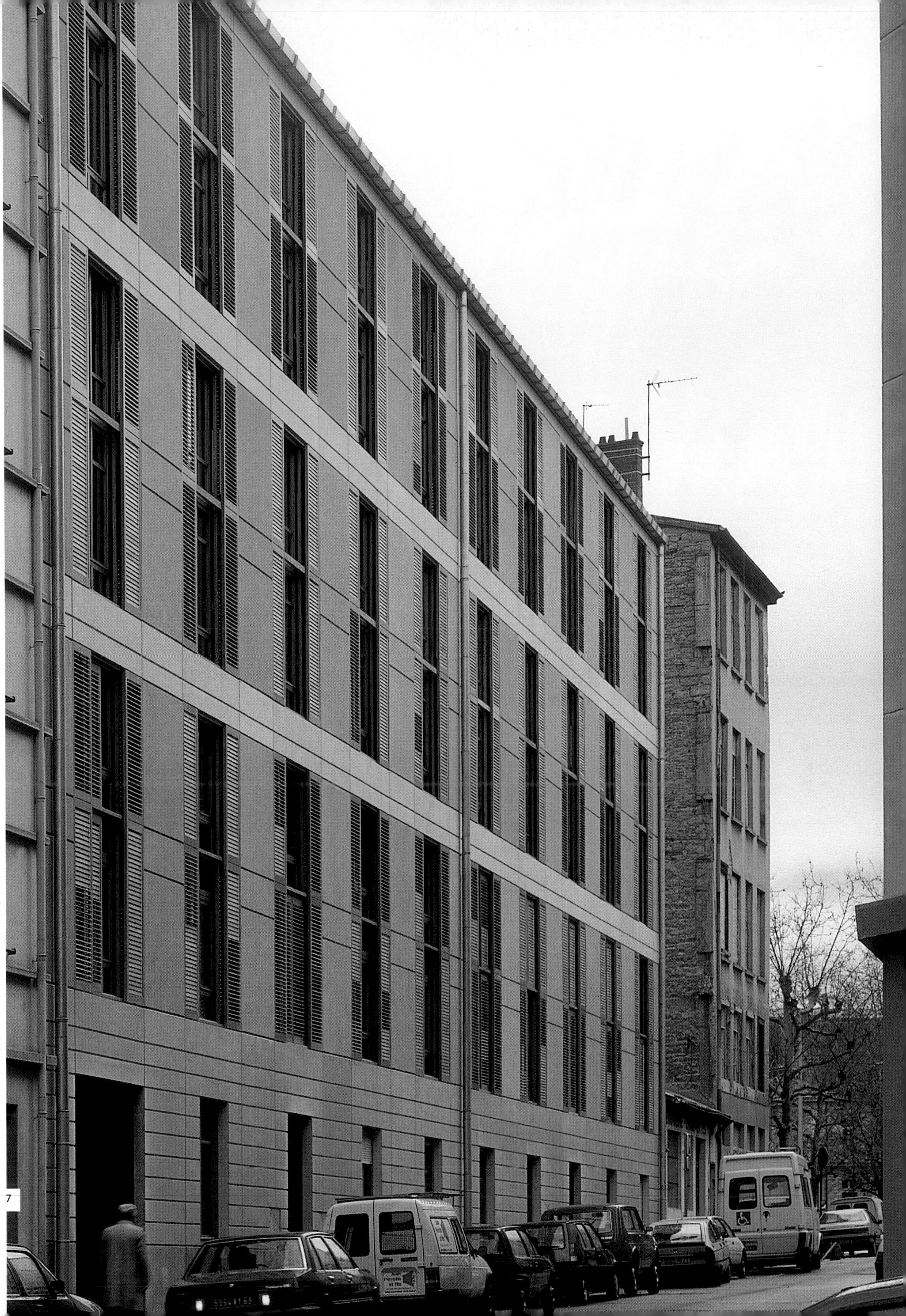

8

9

On these pages, various examples of projects in the historical center of the city. While Jourda & Perraudin have opted for a modern interpretation of the existing façades, Herzog & de Meuron and Souto de Moura have preferred to construct an abstract plane which can be seen as a silent intruder on the existing city.

7. *Apartments in Schützenmattstrasse, Basle, 1993, Herzog & de Meuron*
8. *Dwellings in La Croix Rousse, Lyons, 1994, Jourda & Perraudin*
9. *Dwellings in Ciutat Vella, Barcelona, 1997, Pep Llinàs*
10. *Houses in the Rua do Teatro, Oporto, 1995, Eduardo Souto de Moura*

10

11

14

12

15

13

16

The heart of the city is not just a meeting place, it is also a symbolic image. The decision to build a space of this kind is very much linked to the desire to form a close-knit society. The origins of democracy in Greece are inseparable from the construction of the public space.

11. *Place de la République, Lyons, 1993, Alain Sarfati*
12. *Place de la Gare, Strasbourg, 1994, Gaston Valente*
13. *Place des Terraux, Lyons, 1994, Christian Drevet*
14. *Jacob Jacovitz Plaza, New York, 1995, Martha Schwartz*
15. *Harbour Square, Helsinborg, 1993, Sven Ingvar Anderson*
16. *Place de l'Homme de Fer, Strasbourg, 1994, Guy Clapot*
17. *Plaza de los Fueros, Estella, 1993, Patxi Mangado*

On these pages, various views
of the centers of:

18. *Mexico City*
19. *Nantes*
20. *Frankfurt*
21. *Philadelphia*
22. *San Francisco*
23. *Los Angeles*
24. *New York*

In the cities of south-east Asia, public space is largely dependent on private initiatives. Ground level is dominated by the automobile, with many streets having the appearance of urban free ways, often without pavements.

25, 26.
Views of the centers of Singapore and Hong Kong.

27, 28, 29.
Streets in Nantes, New York and Tokyo

In all three cases, these are well established urban spaces, although the style of the buildings and urban atmosphere are very different. The image of the city is also a reflection of the culture of each country. It is remarkably difficult to import typologies from other places.

30

Cities such as Tokyo and Los Angeles have recently tried to recuperate some areas of their centers in order to construct plazas and public spaces for pedestrians.

30, 31. *Pershing Square, Los Angeles, 1994, Legorreta Arquitectos*

32. *Citizens Plaza, Tokyo, 1991, Kenzo Tange Associates*

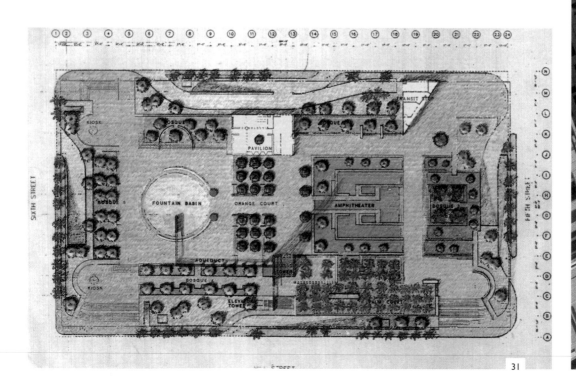

31

Macrobuildings-Microcities

As our great cities have got larger and larger–covering entire regions with their web of infrastructures–their tentacles have encompassed neighboring towns and villages; they have transformed the countryside into industrial estates, and the forests and woods into leisure estates. At the same time, within the city, new constructions have appeared which are more "city-like" than the city itself; that is, they are a distillation and intensification of the concentration which the city symbolizes. Here we have a phenomenon to seduce the imagination of Borges: a superposition of times and scales. The city is, simultaneously, the protagonist of its own end and new beginning. The situation has a certain logic: if the city is essentially concentration and density–as opposed to the expanse of the countryside–it seems normal that, when the urban warp has been stretched to the point where territory and metropolis are synonymous, there will be a tendency for the city to redefine itself in basic terms; once more seeking to be a concentrated space within a dispersed area.

Increasingly, we are witness to the construction of huge buildings whose functions are multiple–shopping areas, internal communications, leisure facilities, offices, restaurants, bus, train or subway stations, interior plazas, gyms, rows of shopping stalls, hotels, car parks, cinemas, repair shops, etc.

Normally, these agglomerations are identified as shopping malls, central stations, airports, convention centers, trade fairs, or international hotels, but the actual name is of minor importance, given that this identifying function is the focus for all the above-mentioned commercial, mercantile, or leisure activities, which represent what is available in what we consider as the "city". Again, if we take into account that the concept of the city is fundamentally one of concentration–of services, activities, and information–, we can say that these great mega-centers are in fact the cities of our time.

What is paradoxical in this explosion of macrobuildings/microcities is how little they have inherited from the traditional city. In addition, they do not grow outside the metropolitan areas, but provide instead a parallel alternative to historical city centers. We often see the appearance of a new shopping mall with a very similar ground plan to a normal city centers–a system of streets with rows of shops, one next to another–while in the same metropolitan area, there is undoubtedly another area with a very similar layout fulfilling exactly the same functions. In this fashion, the newly created microcity imitates, sabotages, and impoverishes the traditional center; the copy substitutes the original, just as David was replaced in the Piazza de la Signoria. As philosophers such as Guy

Melbourne Central Building Plaza. It houses offices, shops, entertainment, restaurants, and a subway station.

1. *Melbourne Central*
   Melbourne, 1991
   Kisho Kurokawa

Schiphol, Amsterdam's airport, has experienced steady growth since its inauguration in 1950, and has become a small city in its own right. When the West Terminal was enlarged, it was decided to give the "city" its own urban center: Schiphol Plaza.

2, 3. *Schiphol Airport*
   Amsterdam, 1993
   Benthem Crouwel NACO

2

3

Macroedifices are difficult to integrate into the city itself, as they are designed to serve a whole region. Their scale is of large territorial infrastructures.

Debord or Jean Baudrillard have noted, this process is one of the constants of contemporary society.

This process of substitution of the city by a building means that its surroundings are converted into the periphery. With the concentration of services within the recently created nucleus, the rest of the area becomes a subsidiary, dependent territory.

It is a very different thing to recreate a model in another, distinct place than to do so in the interior of the original. This second process, rather than being a copy, is more of a simplification or a reduction. To produce the necessary concentration, it is necessary to abandon some element, and here, the housing element is the one being discarded. Although it is true that these great new "containers" are capable of receiving thousands of people each day, very few actually sleep there, and those that do are almost all in transit. This differentiates these new centers very clearly from the traditional city, which not only puts people into contact with each other but also gives them permanent shelter.

This tendency has contributed to the fact that more and more people live outside the city, a shift which should not be surprising if we contemplate prototypical twentieth century cities such as Dallas or Houston, whose downtowns are almost bereft of housing. Even in the great European capitals, the historical, pre-twentieth century center is seeing its occupants disperse to the suburbs, leaving behind offices, shops, and tourists.

In a parallel development, new areas have grown without services, designed only for occupation; just huge, silent dormitories where people go to sleep, to leave again early in the morning. This disassociation between domestic life and public activity results in a degeneration of the city's quality of life, but at the same time it accelerates and

clarifies its dynamics and increases consumption. The equation is not a matter of chance.

Current developments in telecommunications have meant that an ever-increasing amount of activities can be carried out without travelling. Today, shopping, banking, enjoying a football match, and even work itself are activities that can and increasingly are being done at home. This could suggest that these great new service centers are being built in the face of long-term trends. If the dynamics of modern life seem to imply that more and more things are being carried to the domestic unit (whether in real or virtual fashion) it may seem to be flying in the face of the future to build huge centers in order to attract people from their homes. However, it is precisely this tendency to spend more time at home that is accelerating the concentration of services in fewer and fewer places, and thus leading to the construction of the new megacentres. If a family has only one afternoon a week for leisure, it may be preferable to have the supermarket, record shop, restaurant, water fun park, and the cinema grouped under the same roof, in order to compete for the family's valuable time and money. One clue could be that these macroedifices first began to appear in countries with cold climates, where the prospect of walking the streets is less pleasurable, and where people tend to spend more time at home. Their acceptance in Mediterranean countries, for example, has come much later.

Whatever the reasons, it is important to realize how this concentration of services and activities affects relations between individuals in these societies. If all of a person's or family's leisure time is spent in one of these megacenters, they might have no other links with the rest of the citizenry except for those that are purely commercial or work-based. It may be thought curious that in a

society characterized by ever-greater consumption and increased leisure time, both activities are concentrated in the same places. It seems clear that services follow the trajectories people take, with a multitude of parallel services grouped around points that attract people's attention. In this way, the main communication centers and the interchanges of daily life have also become shopping, financial, and leisure areas. The evidence can be seen in the lobbies of the main metro stations in large cities, which house an increasing array of shopping malls and office blocks. A parallel development is the increasing use of airports for business meetings: executives do not have to travel to the heart of the city, but can stay in the hotels surrounding the airport instead, and meet at the convention centers or suites.

In *Tombés du ciel*, a French film made at the beginning of the nineties, Jean Rochefort plays a Canadian who loses his passport during a flight and, on arriving at Charles de Gaulle airport in Paris late on Friday evening, is forced to stay in the airport all weekend, waiting for the consulate to solve his problem on Monday morning. Over the course of the weekend, he meets a series of characters who live permanently in the airport, having no visa to enter France and no permission to return to their own countries. They hunt for rabbits on the runways and sell them to the airport restaurants; they wash in the airport rest room each morning, go shopping in the afternoon, and chat with the passengers in the waiting lounges. In spite of their precarious situation, their lives are organized in a way which mimics that of the inhabitants of the city. All the services they need exist in the airport. Not only large airports but also railway and bus stations are duplicating their functions and becoming hotel and business centers. One of the clearest examples of this trend is the Euralille complex; in just a few

5

6

7

years, a new, parallel city–complete with convention centers, large shopping areas, office blocks, etc.–has been constructed on the outskirts of the historical nucleus of Lille. The city of Lille is an important junction in the new TGV high-speed railway system being extended throughout Europe; it is also the entrance to the underground tunnel linking France and England under the English Channel. This has led the French authorities to promote the possibilities of the city as a business center on a European scale.

These small-scale new "cities", unlike the traditional city, are designed as a whole, unitary concept. In the case of Lille, the participants included some of the most prestigious European architects such as Rem Koolhaas, Jean Nouvel and Christian de Portzamparc, but in too many other cases the architects are neither so distinguished nor so varied; and the criteria followed have less to do with space, urbanism, or the landscape and more with economy and speed of construction. The fact that a single architect or team of architects should be charged with building a whole "city", even on a reduced scale, may give rise to some doubts, although it is not something either new or recent in the history of architecture: from the Renaissance onwards there have been many examples. In this new typology of edifice/city formed by interminable airports and huge shopping malls, the difference is that not only is the urban strategy determined from the start, so too are the building solutions, the choice of finishes, the urban furniture, the general image, and even small details such as the color of the wastebaskets. There is neither the time nor the money to leave anything to chance: the center arises out of nothing in a few years and the inauguration date is untouchable.

The traditional city is characterized by slow and gradual growth covering different historical periods, and encompasses different and even contrary ideas of what the city is; in the new macrobuildings/microcities, the norm is unitary order, one way of working and, above all, an extremely short construction period.

Examples of edifice/cities are comparatively scarce in the history of architecture. Similar proposals are encountered in the work of Fourier and Le Corbusier, but undoubtedly, in both cases there was a socializing motive, far removed from the basically commercial reasons which fire the builders of the great modern infrastructures. Similarly, the Walking Cities designs by the Archigram group or the structures proposed by the Japanese Structuralists and Metabolists in the fifties and sixties have to be considered, although in these cases, what was proposed was simply a different form of urban growth, based on unitary construction forming a network.

What is being brought about with the construction of these new megastructures is a change of scale. The building as we know it no longer exists, and words such as context or surroundings become virtually meaningless. Each of these metropolitan islands could easily be incorporated into one or more planetary cities: the city of airports for travelling; the city of great museums where large scale exhibitions are interchanged; the financial city connecting the headquarters of the top banks. The functions of these new macrocenters tend to by-pass their immediate context and work on a regional or even continental level. In this too, they are in opposition to the traditional idea of the city.

For these reasons it may seem difficult or even banal to judge this type of construction by the same criteria used for the rest of architecture. They have a different scale, not that of a building or of a traditional city. Within the design teams composed of architects, economists, landscapers, and long lists of engineers of every conceivable type, there is an unavoidable division of work which impedes the designer of the constructive details of the building from having access to the conception of the structure, and the lighting engineer is powerless to influence the distribution of space. However, this division of tasks results in the production of a unitary structure, with similar constructive details, coordinated lighting, and a logical distribution of space. The resulting landscape is notable for its calculated homogeneity, in which even the anecdotal and the seemingly random detail have been overseen by the head architect at a scale of 1/200. The concrete finish and the plate glass of the windows are the same at both ends of the building, even if far apart, because, in the end, the builders of both ends are the same people.

Faced with the success of these megacenters, traditional urbanism seems to have only one way to go: the small city. It is unquestionable that the real megacities of our society–Mexico City, Tokyo, Los Angeles, Cairo, Sao Paulo–are suffering from such acute gigantism that they are not only incapable of reacting to problems in a rapid and effective manner but find themselves totally swamped by the conflicts caused by their huge size.

Thanks to developments in communication, the activities and information characteristic of the metropolis can be accessed easily, and at any time, from any small town or village. Equally, the ease of modern travel means that once or twice a year, anyone can travel quickly and cheaply from one side of the globe to the other to see buildings, landscapes, or even a particularly interesting exhibition. The possibilities of success in business are the same regardless of place, if it is well communicated. Today, a city of between a hundred and three hundred thousand people enjoys the same services as a capital of four millions, but only suffers half its problems. A small city can be crossed in a matter of minutes, and reaching the center is child's play, reducing the attractiveness and success of the megacenter alternative. Pollution levels are much lower. The attractive alternative of converting large areas of the city into pedestrian areas is not traumatic, as a large range of activities can be performed without the car. In addition, these cities have sufficient levels of population to ensure a wide range of cultural and social facilities–cinemas, theatres, museums and concert halls–while public services are closer and more accessible to the citizen. Levels of crime are lower and, in contrast with the anonymity of the great city, social relationships are easier and more fluid.

8

7, 8. Stairs, lifts, galleries, and enormous, amorphous rooms dotted with serving counters and small cubicles substitute the traditional street.

In these macroedifices, the roof almost always shows an independent structure which is often spectacular, but born of a contradiction: enclosing the space to protect it from the elements and preserving the sensation of a free, open space at the same time. In many cases, this paradox is expressed by a transparent roof.

9. *Tokyo International Forum, Tokyo, 1997, Rafael Viñoly*
10. *Embarkation Lounge of Pointe-á- Pitre Airport, Guadaloupe, 1996 Paul Andreu*
11. *Foyer of the Osaka World Trade Center, Osaka, 1995, Nikken Sekkei*
12. *Connecting link between the train and tram in Strasbourg, Strasbourg, 1994, Gaston Valente*
13. *Connecting link between the airplane and high speed train in Charles de Gaulle Airport, Paris, 1994, Paul Andreu*
14. *General view of Charles de Gaulle Airport. In the foreground, a hotel lies among the routes which connect the different terminals*

15

The shopping malls often reproduce the form of traditional streets, but it is not very often that the same building materials are used. In the mall, the decoration is more shiny and cared for, provoking a strange sensation of artificiality which makes emotional identification difficult, but facilitates commerce.

16

15. *Nordwest-Zentrum Shopping Center,*
    Frankfurt, 1990
    Rhode, Kellerman, Warwrowsky+Partner

16. *BePop Shopping Center*
    Helsinki, 1991
    Jyrki Tasa

17. *Galerías Lafayette, Berlín, 1996, Jean Nouvel*
18. 19. *Euralille Comercial Centre, Lille, 1994, Jean Nouvel*
    20. *Plaza in the shopping center in Kawasaki station in the Tokyo area, 1995, Nikken Sekkei*
21, 22. *L'Illa, Barcelona, 1994, Rafael Moneo and Manuel de Solà-Morales*
    23. *Stuttgart Airport, 1992, Von Gerkan + Marg*
    24. *Hamburg Airport, 1993, Von Gerkan + Marg*

19

20

41

23

24

25, 26. Macroedifices are always provided with a comprehensive systems of signs and
directions. Even so, it is easy for the visitor to lose his bearings due to the
constant movement of people in all directions.

25

26

The periphery

The periphery is an imprecise place, difficult to define, with no clear boundaries. Moreover, it is often not thought of as a place in itself, but rather as the area where the city begins to disintegrate, scattering bits of urban detritus with no apparent logic. The idea of undefined territory where opposite forms come together (it is not the city, nor can it be called rural landscape or natural environment) is tremendously seductive for current thought and criticism as it is associated with the concept of limits.

Nevertheless, the fact that it is given a name (or several: periphery, outskirts, suburbs) shows that it is a place with certain recognizable and identifiable characteristics which must be studied, catalogued, and ordered. Although the outlying landscapes are extraordinarily diffuse and disconnected, and in spite of not having a defined structure or a coherent image, they constitute an incontestable reality. Therefore, it is necessary to begin to discover and dominate their laws in spite of their complexity.

The extensions, avenues, and plans for growth through grids of streets in Paris, New York, Amsterdam, Barcelona and, in fact, all of the urban transformations of the 19th century, in spite of creating an urban framework completely distinct from the previous, were conceived with the will to create a city and the security that the divergences from a traditional image did not imply a division or fracture.

Similarly, the periphery, although different, constitutes the contemporary city form. Adopting this idea is decisively important to be able to establish urban strategies with no initial errors. As such, the identification of the periphery as the place where the city ends is extremely dangerous. Urbanity can no longer be circumscribed to the historical center with its neat layouts of squares and avenues. Instead, our point of view has to change radically to see that the periphery is where today's architecture is constructing the new city.

Its components are no longer streets, squares, and gardens; rather they are blocks of isolated buildings, highways, junctions, factories, warehouses, toll booths, gas stations, bridges, electricity towers, signs, advertisements, shopping centers, parking garages, airports, telephone wires, telecommunication towers.... The development of communications has brought with it the complete transformation of city scale, which has multiplied and, on occasion, occupied entire regions; a metastasis that creates imprecision.

Old cities and towns maintain their human scale (a pedestrian might still cross them on foot). But the peripheries and congested centers are configured according to the measure of cars, trains, airplanes, and telecommunication networks.

In the periphery, the main mode of transportation is the car, and the freeways structure the territory; the buildings alongside are destined to be seen fleetingly from a moving vehicle, as are the traffic signs and the advertising billboards.

1. *Landscaping along the A.85 highway Angers-Tours-Vierzon, 1997 Bernard Lassus et Associés*

2. *Headquarters of Sun-Aqua TOTO Kitakyuschu, 1994 Naoyuki Shirakawa Atelier*

3. *Le Sémaphore Lyons, 1994 Christian Drevet*

1

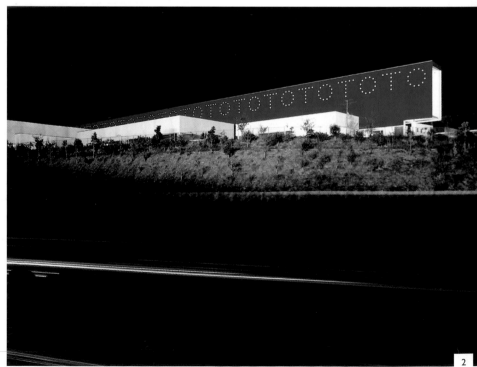

2

Projects like the Nemausus blocks of apartments designed by Jean Nouvel and Jean-Marc Ibos are objectively based on the materials, the images, and the signs of the periphery, and are capable of inventing a new sensibility: the metal railings, the folding, industrial doors giving access to the apartments, the interior scale, the exterior finish of corrugated sheeting, the fanlights painted in red and white like traffic signs.

4. *Nemausus*
Nîmes, 1987
Jean Nouvel/
Jean-Marc Ibos

The job of the architect may be that of giving added meaning to purely technical buildings. Unlike sculptors, the idea is not simply to place a finished work on a site, but rather to appropriate and transform an existing infrastructure or enrich an engineering project such as this public barometer in the suburbs of London.

5. *Thames tower*
London, 1995
Brookes, Stanley, Randall,
Fursdon

Thus, unlike the traditional city, the periphery demands access for vehicles. There is now no direct contact with the immediate surroundings but, in the majority of cases, this relationship is lived through the windshield of the car. Neither are distances the same: a building which seems near at hand may require a longer journey to reach it than another which is a couple of kilometers away. On the periphery, relative distances are conditioned by the prevailing road system.

As our vision of the city is transformed, its constitution also inevitably changes. However, like the majority of long-lasting social phenomena, there is no logical chain which can abstractly explain the process which has taken place. The train, the telephone, television and, above all, the automobile have been the catalysts of this evolution and the image of the peripheral city is, in large part, a result of the laws imposed by these elements. A street of terraced houses with a defined pavement and roadway has meaning from the pedestrian point of view, but much less from that of the motorist. The traffic problems suffered by all our major city centers only go to prove this point. Curiously, one of the solutions sought to this problem has been the incorporation of highways—a traditional element of the periphery—to the center, albeit disguised under the names of ringroad, urban throughway, etc.

The reverse has also occurred. Demographic development and the growth of cities have pushed inhabitants out of the city center, forcing them to make long journeys for shopping or even to see friends. In this way, urban expansion implies a constant need for transportation.

From the moment in which the city dweller is obliged to use his car or the train to get to work from his neighborhood five or ten miles outside the center, it is but a short jump to moving to a house in a nearby country town or by the sea. The daily journey is not much greater, and is compensated by a momentary improvement in quality of life. This is not a hypothesis but a reality which has become only too obvious in all our major cities over the last few decades. Large cities are losing population, while towns situated twenty, forty and even sixty miles away

4

are growing. However, this process leads inexorably to their eventual incorporation into the metropolis as satellite towns (a term previously used only for dormitory towns and suburbs of drab appearance situated on the periphery).

Thus, just as the urban expansion of the last century incorporated the rural towns and villages that surrounded the cities, the expansion of the modern metropolis is devouring whole regions. If a place sixty miles from the center of the city can now be considered as the periphery, the question is; where does the city end? Perhaps soon the answer will be; in the periphery of the nearest adjoining city: metropolis and territory are synonymous, all is city.

If everything constructed is part of the urban weft, classification becomes impossible. There is no contrast between city and country. It is trivial to say that the city has this or that aspect, because in fact it encompasses all existing aspects. The indefinition of periphery becomes the prototype of the city of the future.

The city is still the physical image of the society that constructs it. Without doubt, one of the most widespread modern phenomena is the process through which products, news, and trends reach a mass audience and then disappear without having generated concern for where they came from, where they have gone, or, much less, for the problems left in their wake. One trend immediately succeeds another with no interval, without even a period of consolidation or decline. No justification is needed—it is simply 'in fashion'. By the same token, buildings interrupt the periphery without being adjusted to a previous order and without knowledge of the future of its immediate surroundings. We are frequently witness to some controversy about the construction of a modern building in the old part of a city, but works carried out in the periphery are seldom criticized, even though they are normally less carefully planned. Anything goes in the outskirts.

In a way, this observation reveals more a dynamic and a way of facing the projects, than a common description of the periphery. Any type of activity can develop in the outskirts: industrial, transport, commercial, residential.... In fact, an example of why the

periphery is not a marginal zone of the city but rather the current way to construct is the incorporation of social centers (commercial centers, clubs, museums, workplaces) which are often full of visitors, while the main streets are empty.

The indistinctness of the periphery's overall shape provokes architects into many differing responses, ranging from absolute self-absorption to the will to transmit feeling and lyricism. The common link, regardless of stance, is the difficulty of integration in the surroundings. There is a consolidated landscape both in the traditional city and in nature that invites inclusion in the established

6

7

image. Whatever the case, any transgression is highly obvious and constitutes a point of departure, not an alteration of the whole. Eradication and decontextualization are the common denominators in the periphery.

An architect must almost always confront the problem of scale. Large empty spaces and the obligatory use of the car call for different approaches to the building which include both visitors arriving on foot and by car.

The perception of this is not even direct: reality is a reference, a door which gives access to cinematographic or television images which immediately substitute the real thing. For this reason, a design cannot be generated exclusively through its relationship with the immediate surroundings but must also take account of its virtual surroundings: a landscape which is formed just as much by a petrol station, a discotheque or a solitary block of flats as by a film or an advertisement.

Thus, the building does not suppose an ordering of the land. When planning includes streets and squares, buildings complete an urban plan designed not only to provide routes and distribute the buildings but also to create an urban space. The dispersion and disorder of the periphery convert buildings into images or even the protagonists of a videoclip. Taking this to its logical conclusion, we can see that for the driver or even the pedestrian in the periphery, a traffic sign and the façade of a theatre together form a common landscape in the same way that in the traditional city the grouping together of houses forms a common route. It is becoming obvious that an iconography of the periphery now exists to the extent that there are specific elements and common materials.

Concern about the consequences of an architectural project in the periphery generally centers around its impact on the landscape. Viewing the building as an object, architecture incorporates sculptural techniques.

In fact, modern sculptures are often placed at road junctions to serve as landmarks. Of course, indicating an intersection with a Claes Oldenburg or an Alexander Calder sculpture is, no doubt, not the same as using a sign saying you are at point X or such-and-such street. Besides indicating, a sculpture incorporates added meanings and images to modify perception, which is to say that these isolated performances have the capacity to change an incoherent territory into an emotive landscape.

Just like the red entrance doors of Japanese temples set in the middle of a valley, or Paleolithic menhirs, the overlapping between architecture and landscape creates the potential for a building to become a monument, irrespective of its use. Thus, a paradox arises: the manner of building a contemporary city lies in the capacity to evoke a landscape, whether it be historical, imaginary, or simply lyrical. At a time when the scale of the city is territorial and large-scale urban projects are the construction of roads, railway lines and airports, architecture must adapt to this new scale. Trying to stretch the limits of the traditional city is nothing more than trying to hold back the tide.

The absence of façades and streets means that the periphery is an untidy and dispersed territory. This same spatial anarchy gives more formal freedom and greater tolerance toward all manner of architectural experiments.

6. *Glass House, Hiroshima, 1995, Shinichi Ogawa*
7. *Quarry used to store old cars in Majorca*
8. *Match book, Barcelona, 1992, Claes Oldenburg*
9. *Drama School in the outskirts of Mexico City, 1994, TEN Arquitectos*
10. *Houses at Lake Gooi, Huizen, 1996, Neutelings & Reidijk*

8

9

10

On the preceding pages:

11, 12, 13.
Two bridges on the outskirts of Reykjavik, 1995, Studio Granda

14

Sejima works her façades as if they were a graphic design. The building is converted into a poster with an unusual depth of plane.

14, 15. *Pachinko Parlor II and Pachinko Parlor III, Ibaraki, 1993 & 1996, Kazuyo Sejima*

Noise leads to silence. In contrast to the chaos of signs, objects, colors and forms, buildings possess a rigorous hermetism.

16,17. *Pedestrian walkway, Miami, 1994, Jerry Marston, Wallace, Roberts and Todd*
18. *Stop Line Discotheque, Bergamo, 1996, Studio Archea*
19. *Landscaping along the A.837 highway, Saintes-Rochefort, 1997, Bernard Lassus*
20. *Soundproofing wall, Miami, 1996, Martha Schwartz*
21. *Bielicky House, Düsseldorf, 1995, Wolfgang Döring*
22. *Housing block, Graz, 1994, Riegler & Riewe*

23. *Le Stadium, Vitrolles, 1995, Rudy Riccioti*

24. *Offices for Riddell's, Jackson Hole, 1995, William P. Bruder*

The first buildings to colonize the periphery are warehouses, factories, storage depots, truck-stops, and discotheques: simple and cheap constructions which impose their own aesthetic.

25. *Gran Velvet Discotheque, Barcelona, 1994, Alfredo Arribas*
26. *Shopping Center on the outskirts of Parma, 1988, Aldo Rossi*
27. *Hôtel Industrielle, Paris, 1990, Dominique Perrault*
28. *Railway switch control tower, Basle, 1995, Herzog & de Meuron*
29. *Campus classrooms, Aveiro, 1995, Eduardo Souto de Moura*

Just like the painter who leaves his vision of a place on the canvas, the architect projects his viewpoint onto the landscape. However, unlike the painter, the vision of the architect leaves its mark on the site and becomes part of it.

In her extraordinary design for the boardwalk in Gavà, Imma Jansana limits herself to superimposing a minimal scheme of routes over the landscape of dunes.

1. *Sea-front promenade Gavà, 1994 Imma Jansana*

One of the unanswerable questions to which architects often have to respond consists of something along the lines of, "if such—and—such architect builds a fantastic block of apartments or a wonderful theater, when faced with a commission to build another block or another theater, why not simply repeat the same design?" One could adduce reasons of authorship, of budget, or technical problems, but the only totally convincing reply is that each design must involve an interpretation of the place, the topography, the orientation, the climate, the relationship with neighboring buildings, the pattern of the surrounding streets and its continuation in the interior. No design is repeatable, as the conditions are never exactly identical.

Architecture is the way of seeing the world in spatial and tectonic terms. Every place may be considered in many different ways—through painting, photography, or narration—and each way of seeing produces a discourse which is crystallized using different forms—a canvas, a text, or a printed image.

Architecture is the place seen in terms of space. A place is not the same as a site, which represents nothing more than a perimeter line drawn on a sheet of paper. A place consists of a topography and a landscape, but also brings together a history, a cultural context, a vegetation, a geological formation, an orientation, a geography of sound, a map of aromas.

Unlike other activities, architecture represents the only interpretation of a place whose effects are permanently engraved on the place itself, unalterably modifying it. When we talk of integration in the landscape, conservation of the environment, or interventions in historical areas, it is easy to confuse good design with the invisible wish for everything to stay exactly as it was.

As in all human activities, in architecture it is sometimes better to keep quiet and say nothing. However, the conservationist strategy (or its omission) cannot be allowed to spread uncontrolled. Each society must have the opportunity to experience all facets of

2. *Louis Jeantet Foundation*
   Geneva, 1995
   Domino Architects
3. *Kiro San Ehime*
   Observatory, 1994
   Kengo Kuma
4. *Neuroscience Institute*
   La Jolla, 1996
   Tod Williams & Billie Tsien/Burton Associates
5. *Arken Modern Art Museum*
   Arken, 1996
   Soren Robert Lund
6. *Stiklestad Cultural Center*
   Stiklestad, 1992
   Jens Petter Askim

life and leave testimony of their actions. This reasoning justifies construction in all types of space, even bucolic landscapes and historical places, provided that the intervention establishes a dialogue with the context as it adds an enriching, contemporary viewpoint.

In the last century, architecture schools dedicated themselves principally to teaching styles and typologies. If an architect was commissioned to build a hospital or a church, he might opt for a design based on a panopticon or a basilical floor plan. At the same time, he had to decide, in consonance with the function of the building, whether a Gothic, Romanic, or classical style would be more appropriate. The substitution of this way of looking at buildings represents the very history of architecture during the first half of our century and is familiar to us all.

In contrast, the disappearance of vernacular architecture has received much less attention. The evidence shows that "cultured" architecture has co-existed throughout history with the popular variety. If the first has been employed in the construction of public buildings and the villas and palaces of the wealthy, the second produced the dwellings of the majority of the population, especially in small villages and the countryside, often without the intervention of an architect. Vernacular construction is based on the traditional techniques and indigenous materials which master builders, or even the ordinary people, used to build their houses and dwellings. As a result, their integration with the landscape is exemplary. Immediate reciprocity is achieved when using the resources provided by the surroundings—wood in areas of forest, baked clay in dry, arid regions, stone in the mountains.

If the crisis of eclectic, "cultured" nineteenth century architecture and its eventual disappearance was caused by the critical positions taken up by architects of the modern school, it is logical that the weapons of that battle may be seen in the multitude of publications, manifestos, and records of meetings that have been bequeathed us. There has been no such theoretical opposition to vernacular architecture. In fact, Le Corbusier, together with many other modern architects, defended and praised the Mediterranean building tradition on many occasions and used it as an example against the overloaded works of some of his more conservative contemporaries.

The crisis of vernacular architecture is a result of the industrialization of construction techniques. Nowadays, fewer people in the Western world construct their own house, and if they do, they rarely use the materials of their surroundings, as building materials have become universalized. In Katmandu, as in Seville, it is easier, cheaper, and quicker to build a structure from blocks of reinforced concrete than to use other materials. All building materials—pipes, windows, bathroom fittings, weatherproofing—are factory-made and internationally distributed, either directly, by franchises, or by the delegation of patent rights. The same uniformity that is becoming common in food, politics, fashion, and leisure pursuits has affected the way we construct our buildings. It is easy to show how recent buildings constructed on different continents are amazingly similar, just as the same makes of car or the same jeans adverts can be seen all over the world. What is more, it is not only building systems and materials that have become universal; as Western styles and habits have become universal, there is a similarity in the program as well.

Aside from the variations allowed for climatic differences, the Modern Movement proposed the same architectural language for all the world. Le Corbusier's plans for Rio de Janeiro and Algiers or Sert's for Lima and Havana coincide in their formal aspects. In fact, the diffusion of the Modern Movement under the name of International Style (mainly after the exhibition organized by Henry-Russell Hitchcock and Philip Johnson in the MOMA in 1932) turned a philosophy into a series of stylistic guidelines—sliding windows, open-plan floors, and white facings. In one form or another, all revolutionary movements—formal and aesthetic, as well as political—tend to see their solutions as universal. This led not only the Modern Movement but also the Futurists and the Structuralists to propose decontextualised projects.

In the framework of the productive dynamic of the industrial society, it is more than plausible to envisage the production of mass-produced houses. In fact, the experiments in minimal housing carried out by Hilberseimer and other German architects in the twenties and thirties, are not far removed from this idea. At a time when all kind of electric devices and artifacts such as cars, fridges, televisions, washing machines, irons, and toasters were revolutionizing daily life—along with the appearance of modular furniture, prefabricated rooms, and compact kitchens—it is not surprising that there should have been proposals for completely decontextualised, mass-produced houses, such as the one designed by Buckminster

Fuller in 1927, which he christened Dymaxion House.

Nevertheless, if we understand architecture as the art of constructing places, this definition has no meaning if the definitive location is marginalized. The proposals of Buckminster Fuller and Hilberseimer implied a revolution and, as such, the annihilation of the past. They moved beyond the strictly architectural and became instead the architectonic version of a political ideology.

Although this type of building has met with little success, the research which led to them has produced a completely new residential typology: the motor home. It is logical that the idea of mass-produced houses should give rise to a dwelling where the context (constantly changing) is irrelevant. In addition to trailers and RVs there is also the case of mobile homes (with their element of kitsch) which are carried by truck to their final emplacement. This type of housing is cheaper than a traditional construction, and in some cases is used as temporary housing while the "real" house is being built. Paradoxically, it costs less to import a house from far away than to construct with local materials, a concept unthinkable only a century ago. Thus the new architecture proposed by the theoreticians on the one hand, and the transformation of construction methods and materials on the other, has gradually relegated the vernacular past to oblivion without any significant theoretical or conceptual resistance, or even any wish to do so.

It should be said that many architects, including those within the Modern Movement, have tried to include elements of traditional architecture in their works. The Romantics of the nineteenth century proposed a recuperation of the picturesque—not only in architecture but also in music, folklore, and popular culture—as a strategy to create a national sensibility in opposition to the progressive universalization inherent in the techno-scientific age. However, after the Second World War, the reasons why many architects had to rescue local styles were very different and often diametrically opposed to that nationalism. The desire was to recapture the value of the specific and the disparate in contrast to the uniformity of spirit imposed by the absolutist regimes which brought about the war.

Like an architectural Walt Whitman, the American Frank Lloyd Wright combined modernity with pioneering spirit throughout his work. In the Usonian houses dating from the first decade of the century, but especially with and after Waterfall House (1936), the communion between architecture and nature is evident. Wright built in order to praise the land. In 1908, he wrote of his Oak Park houses: "the Prairie has its own beauty and we should recognize and accentuate this natural beauty, this calm level."

Another fine example of this attitude is the career of Alvar Aalto. This Finnish architect, whose first works, such as Vipurii Library (1927-1935) or Paimio Tuberculosis Sanatorium (1928), were built according to the strictures of the Modern Movement, began to work with materials such as wood and brick at the end of the thirties. He became interested in the texture of finishings, and mixed materials with unusual freedom to

7

produce heterogeneous shapes, which fragment until they become integrated with the scale of the landscape and the individual. Aalto developed an organic architecture of smooth shapes which overcame the right angle and adapted themselves to the surroundings, or the movements of the interior. Just before the War, he finished the Villa Mairea (1938), and after its completion, the MIT dormitories in Massachusetts (1947).

There are many similarities between the work of Aalto and the Mexican architect Luis Barragán, in spite of the differences in climate and cultural context. With his roots also in the Modern Movement, Barragán combines the pure geometric shapes and the chromatic compositions of the neoplasticists with rural Mexican architecture and the landscape. His patios, fountains, lattice-work, cisterns, combined with thick load-bearing walls, and the intense colors of Mexican culture are converted into a surprising repertory of elements which form an abstract and extremely contained architecture. Likewise, Coderch in Catalonia, Fernando Tavora in Portugal, Utzon in Denmark, Tange in Japan,

and even Le Corbusier himself, in the Maison Jaoul (1955) and Ronchamp Chapel, (1955) managed to combine the modern spirit with a desire to recuperate the vernacular.

The revision of tradition carried out by these architects has nothing to do with the reproduction of picturesque images, as it does not spring from a wish to please the client but rather a desire to delve deeply into the possibilities of architecture, in order to integrate with the place.

Currently, there are a multitude of architects whose work reflects this desire: Peter Zumthor in Switzerland, Sverre Fehn in Norway, William P. Bruder in America, Akira Kuryu in Japan, Souto de Moura in Portugal, and Umberto Riva in Italy, among others. Today, too, the boundaries between landscape architecture, or land art, and some strands of architecture are often hazy. Even in contexts where the vegetation or the earth seems more "artificial" than synthetic and prefabricated materials, landscape designers such as Martha Schwartz or Peter Walker are constructing gardens with Astroturf and glass-fiber rocks, while they wait for architecture to be reconciled with nature in those places where it still has some value.

The greenhouse is conceived as the building with the least impact on the landscape. However, in spite of its glass skin, the reflections mean that the volume is seen as a solid mass. For this reason, considerations of profile and shape are as important as in any other building.

8

7. *San Antonio Botanical Gardens, San Antonio, Texas, 1986, Emilio Ambasz*
8. *Graz Botanical Gardens, Graz, 1994, Volker Giencke*

9

The designs of the Japanese architect Akira Kuryu fall somewhere between architecture and landscaping. The use of roof gardens, half-buried elements and façades designed as retaining walls mean that his buildings scarcely seem to emerge from the ground.

9, 10. *Naomi Uemura Museum, Hyogo, 1992, Akira Kuryu*
11. *Okazaki Art and History Museum, Okazaki, 1996, Akira Kuryu*

10

When we talk of respecting nature, we normally think in terms of flora and fauna. However in desert landscapes such as the volcanic island of Lanzarote, integration with the landscape itself continues to be essential.

14. *Timanfaya Park Visitors' Center, Lanzarote, 1993, Alfonso Cano*

Rescuing the tradition of vernacular architecture is just as important as establishing a relationship with the topography.

15. *Manlíu mountain area, La Cerdanya, 1994, Batlle & Roig*
16. *Old people's home, Vantaa, 1993, Heikkinen & Komonen*
17. *House in Tateshina Wood, Nagano, 1994, Yoshihiko Iida*

Various computer images and photomontages of four designs for the center of Manhattan from the Dutch group, West 8. Their designs function in an inverse manner to all the other designs on this page. Here, the architecture does not seek to become integrated in nature, but just the opposite. In today's overwhelmingly urban society, these designs are not just brilliant but, above all, sincere.

18   20

19

21

22

23

24

25

25

26. *Afangar, Iceland, 1990, Richard Serra.*
27. *Iceland Project, Iceland, 1992, Magdalena Jetelová.*

Strategy and Metaphor

In some cases, such as holy buildings –churches, sanctuaries, and cemeteries–, the use of symbols such as the Christian cross is so ingrained as to seem almost indispensable.

1. *Ruidellots de la Selva Cemetery
Girona, 1993
José María Torres and
Enric Serra*

2. *Skulpturdepoter
Ballerup, 1994
Torbe Ebbesen*

Figures related to water and its mythology are often found in fountains.

3. *Plaça de la Constitució,
Girona, 1993
Torres, Martínez-Lapeña
Esteban, Montero, Font*

One of the most attractive enigmas of any creative activity lies in discovering what exactly is the motivating force when one is confronted by the eternal blank page at the beginning of the process. However, unlike writing, music, or painting, in architecture the page is never completely blank. Something previous always exists, whether it be the boundaries of the site, the traces of a path, or the shadow of a tree. In addition, the architect always has a script which must be respected–itineraries to follow, a set of functions to house, an interdependence between the various activities to be distributed in the space. In short, confronted with the blank page, the architect has two supports: the location and the program.

In this, architecture is more akin to photography or cinema, since it is always working with materials that already exist. In photography, leaving to one side strictly technical questions such the control of light and exposure time, the aim is to focus the gaze on trying to capture the emotion of what is being photographed, whether it is a face, a room, or a landscape.

Similarly, the work of an architect does not consist solely of an ordered construction of the spaces specified in the program. Neither is it enough to light them correctly and choose adequate materials that impart a feeling of comfort. In addition to these technical considerations concerning the functionality and solidity of the building, the architect is charged with revealing the spiritual value of each activity.

What differentiates architecture from other plastic arts, such as sculpture and painting, and makes it resemble photography is its capacity for incorporating trivial situations. Like the photographer who roams the city, camera round his neck, searching to trap in his lens an image capturing the magic born from the most anodyne situation, the architect is confronted with the challenge of looking beyond the immediate solution and imparting subtleties to the simplest action.

The task inherent in design is that of foreseeing situations. The architect must reproduce in his mind the itineraries of the users, like a movie sequence. From this point, an interplay is established with the architecture supporting each movement and action, not only from a functional point of view but also psychological, emotional, and architectonic. In order to create a meaning for the form and distribution of the spaces, the emplacement of the windows, and the design of the structure, it is necessary for the user to understand the reasons behind each element.

There is nothing more desolate than a building where it is impossible to find the entrance without asking for help or having to follow signs, or a building where, once inside,

the user loses his sense of orientation and does not know if the entrance lies in front, behind, to the left, or to the right. Increasingly, we see buildings in which the measurements of the windows, the doors, the stairs, and the railings are uniform and standardized. The secret of good architecture lies in precisely the opposite way of thinking: each element should be considered independently after evaluating its specific situation within the building and its relationship with the user.

While visiting some of the houses designed by Le Corbusier, one has the

tury, questions other than the strictly programmatic were more important in defining the shape of a building—the axes, the composition, the symmetry, the rhythm of the openings in the façade, the language of order, the symbolic importance of the façade and the entrance in particular. Uses change but the building remains. If we are guided only by a pragmatic vision, many spaces designed only forty years ago would seem impossibly out-of-date, to say nothing of a fifteenth century construction.

Logically, using a building for a purpose that was not intended supposes some

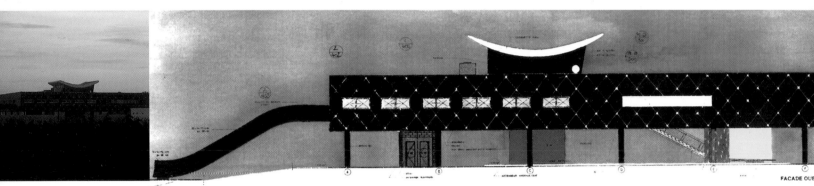

FACADE OUES

unusual feeling that everything is just the right size and that nothing is as it is because it fits into what is "normal". The windows are placed so that somebody sitting can look out and enjoy the view; the shelves are within arm's reach, and the bathrooms emphasize the different functions they fulfill, in a way that allows each to be understood better. At the same time however, there is no exclusive discrimination of the functions: one of Le Corbusier's great obsessions was precisely that of ensuring the flexibility of space and the freedom of the floor-plan. From his very first designs such as the "Dom-Ino" structure (1915) or the Maison Citrohan (1920) he envisaged a dwelling almost bereft of partitions.

It is evident that for a building to function it is not necessary to design exclusively from a functional perspective. In fact, until this cen-

inevitable inconveniences—a fact of life well known to all those who have tried to convert dwellings in the old parts of our cities into offices or shops: no false ceilings or floors to house the installations, immovable load-bearing walls which limit flexible distribution of space, the excessive depth of bays and galleries which makes lighting difficult. However, it is also true that what seem to be the most inconvenient spaces at first, end up being the most used. In the domestic environment, the price of land and commercial considerations mean that each room of the house has an assigned function: bedroom, dining room, kitchen, bathroom, laundry room. Nobody presents a plan with indications such as a very sunny room, or a north-facing room for reading, or ironing, or playing with a train set, or perhaps sitting down with childhood memories on a rainy afternoon. In a society where

5

Both Jacques Fillipi and Santiago Calatrava have produced designs that evoke the shape of an animal. With respect to the young French architect, his building situated in the Camargue manages to transmit the image of one of the typical bulls of the region, while in the shuttle which ferries passengers from the train to their planes at Lyons airport, Calatrava reproduces the silhouette of a bird about to take flight.

4. DRTE Arles, Arles, 1995, Jacques Filippi
5, 6, 7. TGV station at Lyons-Satôlas,
Lyons, 1996, Santiago Calatrava

6

7

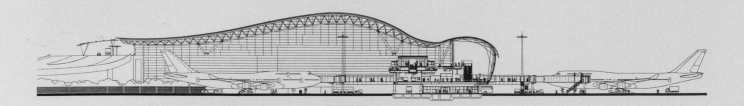

8

people tend to remain in one residence for many years it might be thought more logical not to assign one function to each room forever. This goes to show that talking of functionalism from a pragmatic point of view is very often the worst of errors, although its defenders, those who declaim their "practicality", are convinced of the effectiveness of this approach.

Performance, in architectural terms, does not depend solely on the distribution or assignation of functions, but also involves other, less quantifiable factors such as the placing of a window or the capacity for making the space easily understood.

One of the most ignored and less valued dimensions of architecture is its lyrical capacity. It may seem that something as serious and costly as a building, particularly a large one, cannot be conceived as a metaphor. However, the fact is that architecture is often configured from this point of view, and this is not a recent attitude but rather seems to be cyclical, with various repetitions throughout history. The same metaphors have a new interpretation each time and a different meaning in each building. The pillar as tree is such an ancient image that some would like to believe it predates architecture itself, or rather that the very concept of construction sprang from this image.

Some theorists insist that the Greek temple is a reinterpretation in stone of a simple construction of trunks and branches; otherwise, they say, a system of columns and

beams made of a material so deficient in traction would have no meaning. Thus, the plant metaphor is found at the birth of classic architecture and also in elements of such an apparently contrasting style as Art Nouveau, with Victor Horta's and Gaudí's doors and railings literally reproducing plant motifs.

When Le Corbusier wished to define a new language for modern architecture, his eye settled on boats. His Unité d'Habitation is nothing more than a metaphor of a beached liner, while the TWA terminal at New York's J.F.K. airport evokes a bird lifting its wings in flight.

In recent years, many buildings have been conceived as a metaphor: of a mountain (Denver airport, mansion in Palafolls), a wave (Kansai airport, Domus), a bird (Lyon-Satôlas TGV station), a forest (Stansted and Stuttgart airports), an airplane wing (Lille airport), the keel of a boat (Science Museum in Rotterdam), a leaf (de Menil Collection Museum in Houston), a shipwreck (Arken Museum of Modern Art), television aerials on roofs (square in Parets), a whale (H2O pavilion in Neeltje Jans), an armadillo (Glasgow auditorium), or even more insubstantial concepts such as a rabbit's leap, a dog sleeping, the memory of a river, the sound of the wind, or the smell of wet earth. We may well ask how can anyone design something that evokes a dog sleeping. The answer might well be: in the same way as a poet, a musician, or a choreographer.

One of the greatest engineering feats to take place, as the century closes, has been the construction of an artificial island in Osaka Bay in order to build a new airport. The terminal, designed by the Italian architect, Renzo Piano, is formed by a huge roof in the shape of a wave. Similarly, the roof of the terminal of Denver International Airport, made of stretched canvas, when seen from the sky, resembles the shapes of the nearby Rocky Mountains. When infrastructures become gigantic, architecture seeks refuge in metaphors of the territory.

8. *Side elevation of Kansai airport terminal*
Osaka, 1994
Renzo Piano Workshop

9. *Denver airport*
Denver, 1994
Curtis W. Fentress

10

11

12

13

14

15

17

18

It has become almost commonplace to find the pillars supporting large-scale stations and airports composed of tree shapes. Faced with the amorphous nature of these enormous vestibules, it seems the only possible answer is to adopt the image of the wood or forest. The metaphor is not an afterthought which merely masks the architecture, but rather the motor which drives many of these large-scale projects.

10, 11, 12. *Stuttgart airport*
Stuttgart, 1992
von Gerkan + Marg

13. *Stansted airport*
Stansted, 1990
Sir Norman Foster & Partners

14. *Vénissieux-Parilly metro station*
Lyons, 1993
Jourda & Perraudin

15. *Charles de Gaulle airport train station*
Paris, 1994
Paul Andreu

16. *Pergola designed by Steven Holl*

The Bundestag was conceived as a clearing in the woods: a space which evoked those used for their meetings by the nomad tribes who inhabited Germany twenty-five hundred years ago. These pictures show various details of the vestibule and roof of the Parliament's main chamber. The light seems to shine through the branches of the trees.

17, 18, 19, 20. *German Parliament*
Bonn, 1993
Günter Behnisch

16

19

20

84

21

In front of Barcelona's main train station, Viaplana and Piñón built a plaza which re-interpreted many of the images associated with railways–smoke, electricity pylons, clocks, the movements of the train–from an almost dream-like perspective. Years later, when designing the lighting for a wooden walkway in the port of the same city, they took the undulating profile of the waves as their image.

21. *Plaça dels Països Catalans, Barcelona, 1987, Viaplana y Piñón*
22, 23. *Rambla de Mar, Barcelona, 1994, Viaplana y Piñón*

Arata Isozaki habitually uses metaphors to ensure that his buildings fulfill two conditions: firstly, to present a unified image, and secondly, to integrate with their surroundings. The Japanese Center in Krakow imitates a river; the Palauet of Palafolls a cloud, and his Domus, in its rear façade, reproduces the abrupt profile of the rocks of a quarry, while the front façade resembles the blue-grey crest of a wave.

24. *Japanese Art and Technology Center, Krakow, 1994, Arata Isozaki*
25, 26. *Palauet de Palafolls, Palafolls, 1997, Arata Isozaki*
27, 28. *Domus, La Coruña, 1995, Arata Isozaki*

25   26

Throughout his long career of more than 25 years, the German artist Nils-Udo has developed a literary vision of nature. His designs alter the landscape by the use of poetic images.

29, 30. *Das Talder Blauen Blumen Holland, 1993 Nils-Udo*

31. *Vallée de Bambous Strasbourg, 1994 Nils-Udo*

32, 33. *Landscape with Lake Niederlausitz, 1996 Nils-Udo*

34, 35. *Landscaping of the A29 highway Paris-Le Havre, 1995 Nils-Udo*

The artificial gardens of Martha Schwartz recreate nature using synthetic materials.

36. *The Bagel Garden Back Bay, Boston, Massachusetts, 1979 Martha Schwartz*

37. *Rio Shopping Center Los Angeles, 1988 Martha Schwartz*

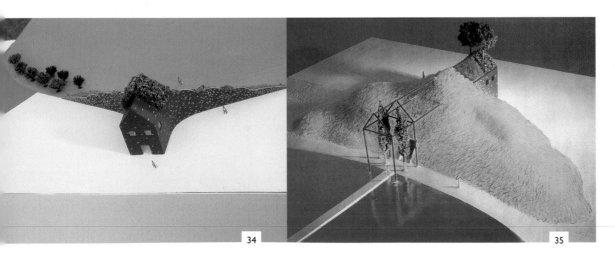

38

Jean Nouvel has imprinted shadows of human figures, which evoke both solitude and overcrowding, over the windows of the Triangle des Gares Shopping Center in Lille.

38, 39. *Triangle des Gares, Lille, 1995, Jean Nouvel*

The lyrical and surrealist constructions of Fuksas, Pei's enormous volumes formed from simple shapes, and Voth's references to the past, represent the best of current trends in monumental expression.

1. *Civita Castellana Cemetery, 1985, Massimiliano Fuksas*

2. *Dallas Auditorium, 1987, I. M. Pei*

3. *Himmelstreppe, Mahra, 1987, Hansjörg Voth*

In 1943, Sigfried Giedion, in collaboration with Josep Lluis Sert and Fernand Léger, wrote the Nine Points on Monumentality:

1. Monuments are human landmarks which man has created as symbols of our ideals, our goals, and our actions. They are destined to survive the era of their construction and become an inheritance of future generations. As such, they form a link between the past and the future.

2. Monuments are the expression of man's highest cultural necessities. They must satisfy people's eternal demand for something to translate their collective force into symbols. The most vital monuments are those which express the feelings and thoughts of this collective force in symbols.

3. Every past era endowed with a real life possessed the force and the capacity to create such symbols. Consequentially, monuments are only possible in eras where a unifying culture and conscience has emerged. Eras which did not rise above the toil of daily life were not capable of creating lasting monuments.

4. The last hundred years have witnessed the devaluation of monumentality. This does not mean there has been a lack of formal monuments or architectural pieces with this aim, but rather that the so-called monuments of recent times have become, with rare exceptions, empty husks. In a way, they represent the spirit and collective feeling of modern times.

5. Decadence and an inadequate use of monumentality are the main reasons why today's architects distrust monuments.

Like painting and modern sculpture, today's architecture necessarily followed a difficult path. It began by solving simple problems, practical buildings such as simple homes, schools, offices, and hospitals. However, currently, architects have reached the conclusion that buildings cannot be conceived as isolated units, but rather must be planned within a wider framework. There is no boundary between architecture and town planning, nor between the city and the region that surrounds it. A reciprocal relationship exists between both. In this type of broader planning, it is the monument which provides the note of color.

6. A new step forward awaits. The postwar changes in economic structures worldwide may lead to the organization of community life in the city, which until the present time has been practically ignored.

7. The people desire that the buildings which represent social and community life offer something more than functional satisfaction.

8. The siting of monuments must be planned. This will be possible when planning of the central points of our cities is under-

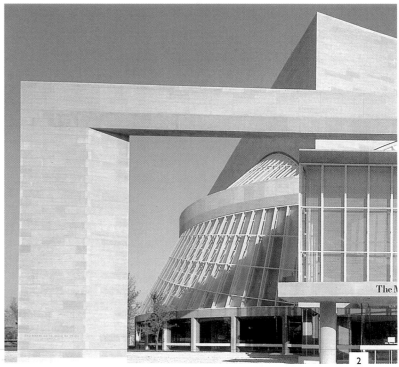

taken with energy. In these open spaces, monumental architecture will find the space it requires.

9. We have modern materials and new technical possibilities at our disposal. New types of materials and new constructions are waiting to be used.

After a period of twenty years during which modern architecture had given a resounding answer to the attempts of totalitarian regimes to introduce their nationalist and fascist symbols into all corners of life, including of course architecture, Sigfried Giedion, one of the theoreticians of the Modern Movement, defendeds the need for a symbolic architecture.

It seems that Giedion had gone over to the other side. It is a fact that the works of Albert Speer, Hitler's architect, or those of Iofan for Stalin, were nothing more than colossal symbolic constructions whose aim was to exalt Nazi and communist ideologies to the masses. However, the architecture that Giedion proposed in his Nine Points on Monumentality was not that of Albert Speer, although it is evident that by 1943 it had been realized that the emotional pulse that had been capable of leading Europe into such a disaster was something completely lacking from the utopia of the Modern Movement.

Undoubtedly, this was one of the most dramatic moments in the history of modernism. Giedion's exercise in self-criticism led him to admit that the lack of concern for the collective will had perhaps indirectly benefited the consolidation of regimes dedicated to exploring the darker side of that same will. At the same time, this was a moment of startling lucidity, as Giedion saw this error not as a failure but rather as a way of enriching the proposals of modern architecture and increasing confidence in its capacity to dignify people's lives.

On the other hand, it is worth pointing out that when Giedion spoke of the essential character of the monument, he was referring to its symbolic dimension, even though the principal quality of a monument is its commemorative function, which is not quite the same thing. The monument tries to imbue the present with the emotion of a past event, although evidently this must be seen in a broad context. For example, the term "historic monument" is something of a tautology, but it serves to shed light on the transformation the concept has undergone from antiquity until the present.

With the invention of printing and the diffusion of the written word, the commemorative function has been assumed first by literature and later by history. This change has not reduced the number of monuments but, paradoxically, increased them. The modern concept of history as a scientific search for the truth, in opposition to the mythological past, has meant that ancient edifices are now seen as evidence of history and, as such, are considered as monuments—even if they are public baths, bridges, walls, or aqueducts; all of them works are whose origin is far from the concept of monumentality.

Today, we are used to using the word monumental not in the sense of a commemorative edifice but rather to signify something colossal, a landmark within the landscape. In this sense, the quantitative aspects become important: the size, the cost, the technical challenge, and the resources used. A work is said to be monumental when its construction implies the employment of a large number of workers and an extraordinary volume of materials. From this point of view, the Tower of Babel would not be monumental because of its symbolization of the integration of different tribes and peoples in one great project, but rather because it implies the participation of such a large number of them in the work. Obviously, one meaning is as good as the other. The fact that one is original and the other modern, or even contemporary, only shows the polysemous nature of the word.

One of the clearest examples of the persistence of the monumental in current architecture is the complexity of great works constructed in Paris during the time François Mitterrand was president of the Republic: the district of La Défense, especially its Arch, the Pyramid of the Louvre, the Bastille Opera House, and the National Library of France. As it has been said on many occasions, Mitterand's wish to perpetuate his memory and leave his mark on history was one of the compelling reasons behind the construction of these buildings. However, aside from any megalomaniac leanings of a national leader, these colossal undertakings have become popular tourist attractions and have served to promote the image of the French capital by adding to its store of emblematic buildings.

Probably, Paris is the city with the most monuments; among others, the Obelisk of the Place Concorde, the Arc de Triomphe, and the Eiffel Tower (originally a temporary construction, its survival due precisely to the wish that it should become a monument), spring to mind without effort. However,

4

A quality common to all monuments is the primacy of idea over form, leading to a frequent tendency to abstraction.

4. *Square in Tel Aviv, 1987, Dani Karavan*

5. *Meseta Library, Los Álamos, New Mexico, 1994, Antoine Predock*

Dominique Perrault's buildings are enormous, impenetrable abstract volumes. The French architect has become weary of repeating that the four colossal towers of the French National Library represent four open books. However, in this project, the symbolic dimension of a political decision of this nature—gathering all knowledge—and the sheer size of the work overshadow the metaphor.

6. *Center of Book Technology Bussy-Saint-Georges, 1995 Dominique Perrault*

7. *French National Library, Paris, 1997, Dominique Perrault*

Parisians are the first to understand that modern tourism needs a strategy of continuous promotion, constant renovation of what there is to offer.

The new monuments of Paris represent an extension of the existing patrimony in a very literal sense. The glass pyramid designed by I.M. Pei as the entrance to the Louvre is obviously an extension of the museum, and a large part of the additional surface area is dedicated to souvenir and book shops, selling all types of objects such as photos, books, videos, key rings, etc., which glorify the museum itself. Likewise, the huge urban operation of La Défense is sited at the prolongation of the main monumental axis of Paris which unites the Louvre with the Arc de Triomphe; also, the principal landmark of the new district is a contemporary revision of the Arc de L'Étoile itself.

In the same fashion, two of the other cultural and touristic landmarks built in Paris during this period, the Bastille Opera House and the Gare d'Orsay Museum are substitutes for other existing buildings: Garnier's Opera House and the Jeu de Paume. Without going into a discussion of their

somewhat dubious architectural quality, it can safely be said that the main intention of both buildings was not to promote culture as such but to construct larger and more monumental "containers", as the contents, the cultural function, remain the same.

In spite of the untold millions invested, there has been no significant urban remodeling of the city. Instead, the option chosen was that of inflating the monumentality of the buildings, as if they were merely balloons. The French have done nothing more than highlight the touristic delights of their capital. All these new works are monumental solely with regard to their gigantic size.

However, the case of the French National Library is somewhat different. Here, for once, it is the concept and the symbolic dimension of the work that is primordial. In some ways, it can be seen more as an ideological exercise than as a cultural facility. In the era of the media, the library was built to contain all information, which means all the power and all the possibilities of creating an alternative power. The four great towers alongside the River Seine symbolize the French desire for power, the real basis for the

colossal size of the building.

In a way, there is a similarity between Mitterrand's great building spurt and that of the Chinese Emperor who constructed the Great Wall. This Emperor wished his reign to be the start of a new era, and tried to eliminate all references to past times: all those caught with old books were deported and forced to participate in the construction of the wall intended to protect the new Empire. Mitterrand decided to crown his presidency by inaugurating a building whose intention was to enclose all literature.

The function of the library as a research center is clearly subordinate to its political symbolism. Ironically, modern technology ensures that access to information does not now depend on its physical accumulation.

This example maybe seen, however, as a unique and special case. The growing importance of tourism in the world economy ensures that it is not the representational possibilities of architecture in the commemoration of an event or the diffusion of an idea that matters, but the capacity to capture publicity instead. The monument has passed from being a symbol to being a mere sign.

Today, to be effective, a monument must be photographed and its image reproduced on the posters of tourist agencies, in tourist guides, on postcards, and in the background of the photos in the family album. Just as our great cities trust the media projections of their monuments to underwrite their tourist promotions, the same thinking has led banks and large firms to build spectacular and charismatic skyscrapers. The constructive dynamic of a city such as Hong Kong, which in recent years has seen the construction of huge buildings like Norman Foster's Hong Kong and Shanghai Bank, I.M. Pei's Bank of China, or Rocco Sen-Kee Yim's Citibank, may be compared with those of Tuscan cities in the fifteenth century, whose noble families competed to see who could build the highest and most imposing tower. After five hundred years, architecture still serves as a way of demonstrating wealth and power. This urban architecture composed of the superimposing of huge exclamation marks evokes nothing and is symbolic of nothing. On the contrary, it seems to be crying, "Here I am! See how grand and powerful I have become!".

What distinguishes sign from symbol is that the first identifies situations or places while the second provokes meanings. One of the causes for the change in significance of monumental architecture is its substitution by other forms of art. In his classes on aesthetics, Hegel explained that, while in primitive civilizations architecture was the main form of symbolic representation, in classical Greece this function was assumed by sculpture, and in modern society it is the written word. The hegemony of one form does not imply the disappearance of the others, but does induce a certain degree of dependency. In classical Greece for example, architecture, in the form of the temple, served to shelter a statue which represented a god, thus creating a meaning. In this way, architecture, although maintaining an important cultural presence for the Greeks, became dependent on sculpture.

Undoubtedly, Hegel would agree that in our present-day society, it is the reproducible image which holds sway over all other forms of representation. Photographs of paintings, reproduced in catalogues, magazines, books, posters, and T-shirts, and whose licensing rights generate huge incomes, have become more important than the paintings themselves. Perhaps not coincidentally, the majority of new art forms such as the happening or landscape art are based on photographic testimony.

The primacy of the reproduced image has had many consequences for art, ranging from total rejection—which has led artists to emphasize the irreproducible, such as Dubuffet's textures or the huge size of Schnabel's work—to the collaboration and complicity in the reproduction of the work itself displayed by artists such as Warhol.

One consequence of this change has been the liberation of art from the confines of the gallery. If Duchamp placed a urinal in an art gallery with the objective of converting it into a work of art, an inverse tendency is now common: happenings and landscape art convert the street or the landscape into the stage for art, bypassing the gallery completely.

The works of Christo, Andy Goldsworthy, Nils-Udo, Ana Mendieta, and Magdelena Jetelova are today's ephemeral monuments—a paradox indeed, but how else can one define an operation like wrapping the Reichstag for two whole weeks? If we take into account the fact that the financing of the project was assumed by the artist himself, using the proceeds from the sale of photographs and videos, it is plain that the essential function of Christo's work was commemorative and thus, monumental.

Similarly, the works of Richard Long or Richard Serra can, in some ways, be likened to the megalithic monument. Although separated by five thousand years and completely different worlds, it is clear that in both cases there is a wish to recover at least part of that spiritual force. Likewise, specific current architectural projects, such as those of Herzog & de Meuron, succeed in converting the architectonic object into a kind of black hole in the landscape, capable of swallowing and reflecting sensations; thanks to an extraordinary geometric simplicity and the meticulous care taken with the skin of the building.

Post-modern architecture has tried to rescue the symbolism of the past by means of a literal recuperation of forms.

8. *San Francisco Modern Art Museum, San Francisco, California, 1995, Mario Botta*

9. *Monterrey Central Library, Nuevo León, 1994, Ricardo Legorreta*

10. *Denver Central Library, Denver, Colorado, 1996, Michael Graves*

The severity and forcefulness of undressed concrete makes it ideal as a material for monumental construction.

11. *Chikatsu-Asuka History Museum, Osaka, 1994, Tadao Ando*

12. *Journalism Faculty, Pamplona, 1996, Vicens & Ramos*

13. *Shoji Ueda Photography Museum, Tottori, 1995, Shin Takamatsu*

14. *Princess Sofía Park, La Línea de la Concepción, 1997, Elías Torres & José Antonio Martínez-Lapeña*

10

11

13

12

14

15

16

17

The projects carried out in Paris during François Mitterrand's presidency were destined to increase the monumental patrimony of the French capital. French *grandeur* has been multiplied to produce a media event which serves to maintain the enormous inflow of tourists to Paris. Similarly, after the fall of the wall, German reunification and the transfer of capital from Bonn to Berlin, the main symbolic act has been the re-vindication of the old Reichstag, first through Christo's "wrapping" and later with the reforms carried out under the direction of Norman Foster.

15. *Pyramid of the Louvre, Paris, 1987, I.M.Pei*
16. *General view of La Défense, the recently created district in Paris*
17. *Wrapping of the Reichstag, Berlin, 1995, Christo & Jean-Claude*

Land Art has managed to recover a certain quality of monumentalism in order to emphasize an empathy with the landscape.

18. *Coups de Sonde, Karuizawa, 1990, Hiroshi Nakao*
19. *Herring Island, Melbourne 1997, Andy Goldsworthy*
20. *Installation in the Parc del Laberint, Barcelona, 1990, Joan Brossa*
21. *Papago Park, Phoenix, 1992, Steve Martino*
22. *Design for Tindaya, Fuerteventura, 1996, Eduardo Chillida*

18

19

20

21

Skyscrapers express a desire for power. The struggle to build the highest building has an immediate and obvious symbolic content.

23. *Melbourne Central, Melbourne, 1991, Kisho Kurokawa*
24. *Petronas Towers, Kuala Lumpur, 1997, César Pelli*
25. *World Trade Center, Osaka, 1995, Nikken Sekkei*
26. *General Bank Tower, Rotterdam, 1992, Murphy & Jahn*
27. *Hotel de les Arts, Barcelona, 1992, S.O.M*
28. *Plaza Centenario, São Paulo, 1995, Carlos Bratke*

26

27

28

Glass has ceased to be a synonym for transparency. The most extreme illustration of this is the Neanderthal Man Museum in the German town of Mettmann, where glass has been used to dress an interior concrete wall.

1. *Neanderthal Man Museum*
Mettmann, 1996
Zamp Kelp, Julius Krauss,
Arno Brandlhuber

2. *Pathé Multicinemas*
Rotterdam, 1995
Koen van Velsen

Transparency has been one of the ideals of architecture over the last two centuries. The capacity to manufacture bigger and bigger sheets of glass and developments in metal structures have led to an explosion of architectural designs based exclusively on these two materials. The "Glass House" or "Crystal Palace" were, until comparatively recently, images associated with children's stories or some kind of imagined Utopia. Today, one has only to walk down the street to see buildings shaped entirely with glass.

During the first decade of this century, an alternative movement of German architects proposed the beginning of a new era of glass-built constructions which would lead to a revolution in social customs. They believed that transparent houses, offices, and workshops would bring about a more open and sincere society. This group, whose principal leader was Bruno Taut, but also included Walter Gropius, Max Taut, Wassili Luckhardt, and Hans Scharoun, engaged in a lengthy correspondence that expounded their utopian proposals, which received the name of *die Gläserne Kette* (the Glass Chain).

For a time, in 1919, Mies van der Rohe was also related to the Glass Chain, as a result of his participation in the radical Novembergruppe. However, in contrast to the visionary creations of the Expressionists, Mies' evolution first led him to adopt the

supremacist and neo-plastic language of Barcelona Pavilion in 1929 and Brno house, and later to create a new classicism of glass and steel during his American period.

As has often been said, and as he himself pointed out in the famous phrase "less is more", Mies' work, rather than an attempt to construct what is apparent, is just the opposite. The final objective of his buildings, with their great steel porticos and enormous expanses of glass, is that architecture disappears. Farnsworth House is a paradigm of this vision: it reduces the dwelling to the construction of two planes—the floor and the roof—and a barely perceptible skin of glass, with the structure disguised as woodwork and all the furnishings grouped in one sole central unit.

Mies navigated between the pull of the vacuum and the exploration of the absolute. The vehemence with which he defends the skeletal, transparent purity of his buildings contains more than a little mystic nihilism. His constructions of glass and steel are, on one hand, a sublimation of technique, while on the other they represent the desire of architecture to cease to be material and enter a spiritual realm.

In fact, the first glass and steel buildings came into being precisely when it was decided to not construct a building. Specifically, the Crystal Palace (1851) was a provisional edi-

fice built for an exhibition: it was decided to erect a metal structure with a glass skin that would enclose a vast space and protect it from the elements, and which would save the cost of erecting a conventional building. Logically, not being considered a building, it was to be dismantled at the end of the exhibition.

In a way, the objective of this type of glass skin is precisely to make architecture disappear. The transparent skin protects from the cold and the rain, making traditional houses unnecessary and allowing life to be lived in the open. The ideas encapsulated in the Crystal Palace were amplified in the geodesic domes designed by Buckminster Fuller during the fifties, and more recently, the designs of Emilio Ambasz such as the planet-building for the Biosphere scientific experiment, which are a reinterpretation of the same idea. It is no coincidence that one of the architects who has given a new impulse to the extensive use of glass is Norman Foster, since he had a close relationship with Buckminster Fuller during the fifties.

Without doubt, however, the glass building that dominates the second half of the twentieth century is the office building, and more specifically, the skyscraper. The enormous towers which occupy the centers of our cities are a paradigm of modern architecture: free floor plan, independence between pillars and walls, and flexibility. The typical skyscraper comes very close to what would be achieved by placing thirty or forty Farnsworth houses one on top of the other.

However, as Mies himself realized when he was working on the unconstructed design for the Friedrichstrasse office tower in Berlin in 1921, the principal quality of glass façades is not the transparency or even the play of shadows but rather the reflections. As everybody knows, it is impossible to see through a window when the sun hits it directly. Another factor is the excessive solar radiation caused by great expanses of glass, which has led to the use of reflecting glass or color filters, which have the effect of making the interior space completely inscrutable.

In recent years, then, glass has been used as an element that can be either transparent, translucent, or completely reflective; the material's ability to play with images is extraordinary; the figure we see in the glass may be behind or in front of it, completely defined or in shadow. This superimposition of planes and images has perhaps been interpreted in Japan better than anywhere else, maybe due to the fact that traditional Japanese architecture, constructed with mov-

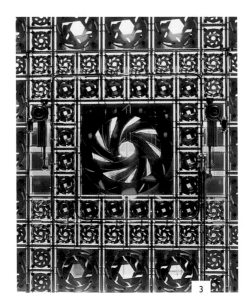

ing partitions and shoji screens, is closely aligned with this dimension of lightness and evanescence.

It is paradoxical, in current architecture, that glass is used to achieve opacity. Architects such as Toyo Ito, Kazuyo Sejima, Gigon & Guyer, Herzog & de Meuron, Wiel Arets, Peter Zumthor, and Fumihiko Maki have contributed to the development of an architecture that is luminous and hermetic, thanks to the use of acid-washed glass or sheets of translucent polycarbon.

The substantial technical changes experienced by the glass industry in recent years have been accompanied by new research into double glazing and the control of sunlight, and today, many new buildings contain various layers of glass automatically regulated by photoelectric cells which control the heat and light levels. In addition, the silicone used for today's glass is capable of supporting much greater forces than before.

However, this substitution of transparency by superimposing filters, although it reflects technical evolution, is, above all, an aesthetic transformation. Virtual reality, conditioned by the simultaneous use of various screens with different layers of images and the superimposing of simulated sequences, the extended use of video and photomontages, which mix reality and fiction, have contributed to producing a voluntarily undefined perception which has affected our way of

Absolute transparency is one of the utopian limits of architecture.

3. *Window of the Institute of the Arab World Paris, 1987 Jean Nouvel*

4, 5, 6. *Various details of the House of Wind and Water Shizuoka, 1995 Kengo Kuma*

seeing the world and constructing it.

In a way, this urge to create complex images has its origin in the reduction of reality to the purely visual. From the moment in which other parameters cease to be important, the work of the editor, designer, publicist, or architect becomes almost exclusively focused on the image, and the loss of other qualities is compensated by a greater visual complexity.

In recent years, the dominant subject in architecture has been the design of the skin of the building, not only regarding the composition of the façades but, above all, the experimentation with materials and systems that convert a simple plane into a much richer space. One of the great novelties in this change has been the incorporation of time as a factor in the design. Façades change according to whether it is night or day, sunny or cloudy, when someone walks behind, or when advertising is displayed. The south façade of the Institute of the Arab World in Paris is a prime example of this; designed by Jean Nouvel, it is composed of metallic latticework evoking the geometric decoration of Arab architecture, and it is electronically programmed to open and close depending on the exterior light.

These new incorporations will surely transform architecture in the coming decades, as altering the limits of a space also means changing the space itself.

4

5

6

The combination of glass with other materials allows the construction of successive skins, thus giving greater depth to façades.

7. *Congress Hall, Lille, 1994,*
   Rem Koolhaas

8. *Museum of Fine Arts, Lille, 1997,*
   Jean-Marc Ibos & Myrto Vitart

Both blocked glass and the acid-washed variety allow glass façades to let light in without being transparent, thus enhancing intimacy and isolating the interior from the exterior.

9. *Block of apartments*
   Tilburg, 1994
   Wiel Arets

10. *Finnish Embassy*
    Washington, 1994
    Heikkinen & Komonen

Fumihiko Maki uses acid-washed glass as if it were a shoji –a traditional Japanese screen.

11. *Church of Christ*
    Tokyo, 1995
    Fumihiko Maki

12. *Lagertechnik offices and garage*
    Wolfurt, 1994
    Baumschlager & Eberle

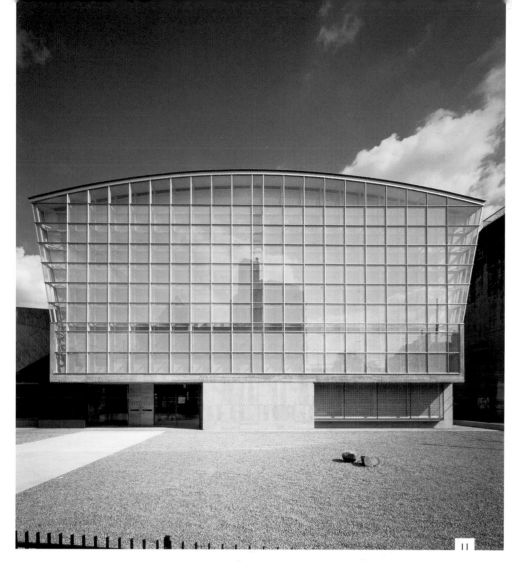

11

12

The vocation of the Cartier Foundation seems to be to merge with the sky, almost to cease to exist. The planes of glass extend beyond the sides and above the building, the metal structure soars through the air without supporting anything. Like a Giacometti figure, Nouvel's building seems not to know if it has just become a solid object or is on the verge of disappearing.

13. *Cartier Foundation*
Paris, 1994
Jean Nouvel

The New Trade Fair in Leipzig is, without doubt, the edifice with the greatest expanse of glass constructed in recent years. In a way it is a continuation and modernization of a tradition which began with the building of the Crystal Palace in the nineteenth century.

14. *New Trade Fair
Leipzig, 1997
Von Gerkan + Marg*

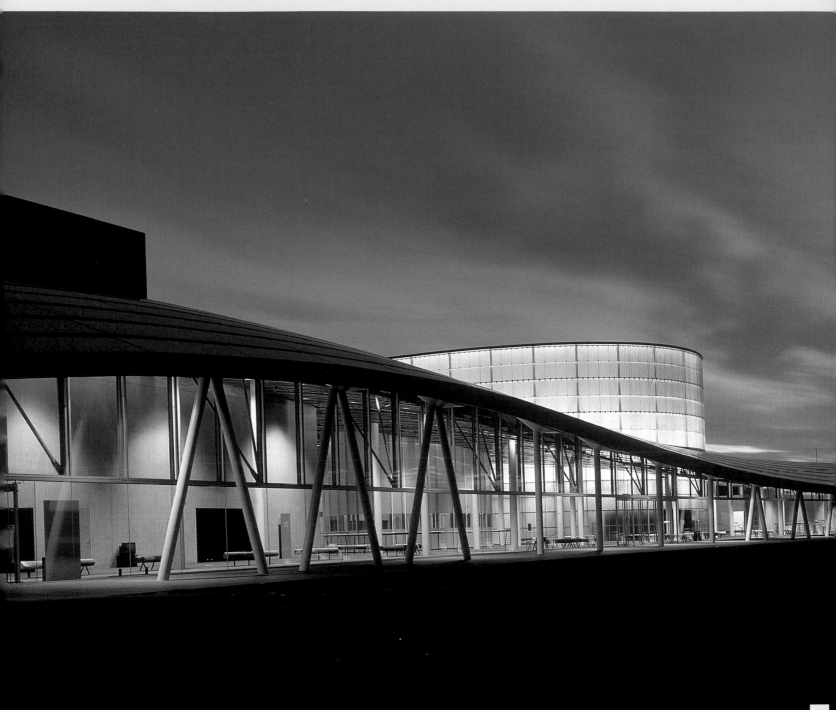

The work or the Japanese architect Toyo Ito is very much influenced by the visual arts. He uses translucent glass to turn the surfaces of his buildings into screens across which shadows of objects and passersby move.

15. *Nagaoka auditorium*
Nagaoka, 1997
Toyo Ito

16, 17. *S House*
Ozumi, 1995
Toyo Ito

The use of slat windows converts façades into elements with a greater variety–from absolute hermetism to almost complete transparency.

18. *Railway signal box*
Basle, 1995
Herzog & de Meuron

19. *Geoscience Institute of the University of Aveiro*
Aveiro, 1995
Eduardo Souto de Moura

20. *Les Chartrons Residence*
Paris, 1994
François Marzelle, Isabelle Menesca, Edouard Steeg

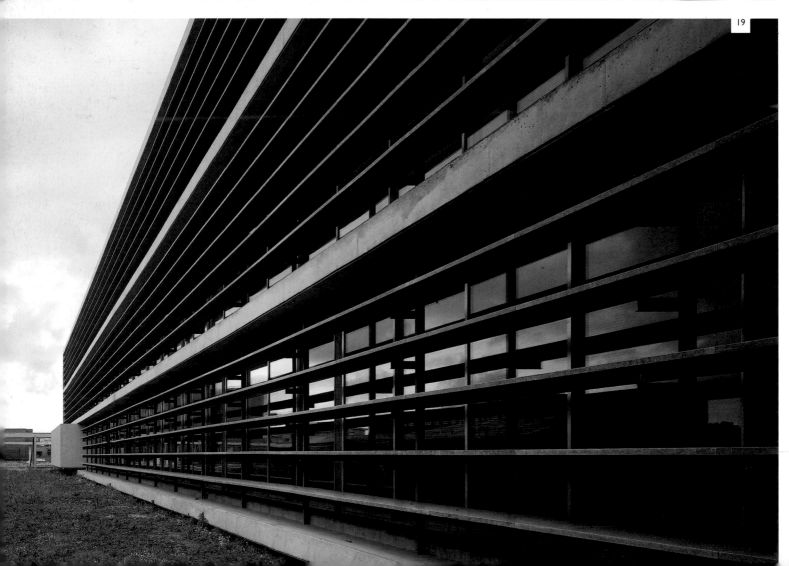

The elimination of any vestige of transparency means the loss of the visual interplay customary in older buildings, which in turn promotes the material qualities of the architecture and the texture of its elements.

21. *New World School, Vienna, 1994, Adolf Krischanitz*
22. *European Design Institute, Vienna, 1995, Ortner & Ortner*
23. *Le Stadium, Vitrolles, 1995, Rudy Ricciotti*

The logic of the structure

3

One of the recurring questions architects are faced with is "Architecture–art or science?" In classical Greece this dilemma did not exist, as the term for art–*techné*–was also used for any other activity destined to produce an object. The concept was closer to what we might define as craftwork, seeing the artisan and the artist as one and the same. At the time of the Renaissance, all artists worked to commissions, with a contract which specified all the details of the work. The concept of art as something belonging to the world of ideas or the spirit has developed comparatively recently, over the last three to four hundred years. In fact, even today, the idea of art as craft is still widely extended: for many people, a painting is good not because of what it suggests or groups together on the canvas, but because it is "well painted". Paradoxically, the artisanal quality of art is also something prized by many current artists, but with a different sense. In contrast to the intellectual claims of conceptual art and installations, many painters defend the concrete, material quality of their work, full of accidents and contingencies imposed by the pigments and the canvas.

When asking whether architecture is art or science, another implicit question emerges: is architecture concerned with the beauty of the building or merely with its structural solidity? Beauty can be taken to mean the composition, proportions, symmetry, and plastic qualities of the work, while solidity concerns the firmness of the structure, its durability, the acoustic and thermal qualities, in short, whether it is "well built". Although this may seem a somewhat puerile distinction, in fact it has solid historical roots.

In the seventeenth century there was a great debate about whether the society of the time had progressed with respect to the classical civilizations or not, a debate which involved some of the most respected thinkers in Europe. The conclusion was that while in some activities, such as sciences and technology, it was possible to see clear progress, in others, such as the arts, the debate was little more than meaningless. This division led to a separation of the teaching of construction into schools of Fine Arts and polytechnic schools. In the first, composition was studied and Greek capitols were drawn and studied, while in the second, forces and the resistance of materials were the order of the day. The consequences can be seen today in the still-existing division between architects and engineers.

In the majority of projects, architects and engineers work together. Architects, even if they cannot calculate the thickness of beams or the diameter of pillars, have sufficient knowledge of structures to allow them to

If the last two hundred years have been dominated by a techno-scientific vision of reality, it might seem logical that the aesthetic of the machine should also predominate.

1. *Institute of the Future
Jaunay-Clan, 1987
Architecture Studio*
2. *La Venerie residential complex
Montargis, 1994
Dubosc & Landowski*
3. *Office block in Minami-Ohi
Tokyo, 1994
Sakakura Associates*

design plausible buildings. The engineers—whether of structures, façades, air conditioning, electricity, or hydraulics—act as specialized consultants. Due to the constant development of technology and the continuous appearance of new systems and solutions in each discipline, the scientific knowledge necessary for the construction of a modern building is, simply, beyond the capacity of any one person. The architect acts as the conductor of the orchestra, trying to adjust and synthesize the input of various collaborators to his particular interpretation of the "score".

However, even today, there are many cases in which this collaboration is not necessary. Sometimes the technology required is so simple that an engineer is not needed. Conversely, the project may be so technical that it consists—like some bridges or communications towers—of a structure and nothing else.

The divorce between the artistic and technical traditions within architecture became particularly evident in the nineteenth century. First, the industrial revolution, with the development of metallurgy and the invention of reinforced concrete, provided unconsidered possibilities and new challenges for builders. Then, architecture became lost in a labyrinth of languages, styles and typologies which, in spite of a tendency towards systemization and rationalization, distorted the images of many buildings.

Iron became a feature of construction at the end of the eighteenth century, thanks to the pioneering efforts of Abraham Darby, John Wilkinson and Tom Paine, who were responsible for the first cast-iron bridges in Coalbrookdale in England and Schuylkill in America. The use of reinforced concrete began in France midway through the nineteenth century, thanks to the parallel efforts of Haussmann's engineer François Coignet, Joseph Monier and, later, François Hennebique.

Two buildings which serve as a paradigm of the period are the Palais Royal in Paris (1829) and St. Pancras station in London (1865-1875). In both cases, the technical skill that went into the construction of enormous glass and iron roofs is covered by a neoclassical façade in the case of the French building and a neo-Gothic one in St. Pancras. The external and internal aspects of the buildings are thus completely opposed. This phenomenon is by no means confined to these two examples but can be found in buildings of this period in the majority of European cities

4

as well as many places in the eastern United States.

When it is said that many current architects, in particular those bearing the label "high-tech", are trying to recuperate the engineering traditions of the nineteenth century, buildings such as Paxton's Crystal Palace or the Eiffel Tower are cited as references. Furthemore, it is often conceded that these buildings, and not the eclectic constructions of Garnier, Pugin or Schinkel, are the real architecture of the nineteenth century.

In effect, it was the designs for bridges, warehouses, factories, stations, towers, and pavilions for fairs that were drawn up by engineers employing the latest technological developments. In particular, the temporary edifices of the famed world fairs were buildings that attempted to demonstrate the scope of scientific development. The most famous building of the last century, the Eiffel Tower, was conceived as a temporary structure for the world fair of 1889, and its beauty was not apparent to all at the time. Guy de Maupassant, for example, considered it horrible, and jokingly remarked that he lunched daily in the restaurant on the upper floors, solely because it was the only place in all Paris from which he could not see the Tower and eat in peace.

During the period dating from Maupassant's anecdote to the construction of the Maison de Verre in Paris's Rue St. Guillaume by Pierre Chareau (1928-1931) (a eulogy to the incorporation of the aesthetic of technique to the domestic space), a slow but sure change of sensibilities took place. These years had seen the development of the artistic avant-garde: Loos wrote, "orna-

mentation is a crime", while Marinetti was of the opinion that "a locomotive in movement is more beautiful than the Victory of Samothrace"; Le Corbusier published *Vers une architecture* and built L'Esprit Nouveau pavilion while Gropius founded the Bauhaus and designed its headquarters in Dessau.

The idea of progress and confidence in the messianic character of the techno-scientific revolution and its capacity to change the world and create a better society crystallized in a revolution in aesthetic sensibilities during the first half of the twentieth century, but these same ideas entered into crisis after the Second World War. If science is capable of discovering penicillin and thereby saving thousands of lives, it is equally capable of inventing the atomic bomb and so bringing death and destruction to a comparable number of people. Technology should participate in democratic culture, and nowadays it is even recognized that it should be "clean" and respect the environment.

In this revaluation of the engineering tradition within architecture, the figure of Buckminster Fuller, the American builder famous for his geodesic domes, is a fundamental one, not only for his own work but also for his influence on his students and collaborators—the English group Archigram, the theorist Reyner Banham (*Theory and Design in the First Machine Age*), and the architects Cedric Price and Norman Foster among them. Perhaps the most emblematic design representing this recreational vision of technology prevalent in the sixties was another Parisian building, the Georges Pompidou Center designed in 1971 by the Englishman, Richard Rogers and the Italian, Renzo Piano.

The English metallurgic tradition has influenced the so-called High-tech movement, whose roots lie in the above-mentioned figures, and which has had such a resounding impact on British architecture in the seventies, eighties, and nineties. Not only Norman Foster and Richard Rogers but also Michael Hopkins, Nicholas Grimshaw, William Alsop, W.S. Atkins, Terry Farrell, Ian Ritchie, John McAsland, and Future Systems have been commissioned to design the most important and flamboyant public buildings in Britain. High-tech architecture is based on the design of a structure and highly technological construction details, which mostly consist of tied steel structures and façades of

sheet metal and glass. As in the great Gothic cathedrals or the Eiffel Tower, the image of the building is born of its technical solutions.

Many of these British architects have, with time, become internationally recognized and their practices have become multinational companies with offices throughout the world. A large part of this prestige is due to the invaluable collaboration of the consultants of Ove Arup Associates, a London firm whose engineers have provided the structure, and often the installations and the acoustics, of the majority of the great high-tech buildings.

However, High-tech is not solely a British movement. Architects such as Renzo Piano in Italy; Frei Otto, Thomas Herzog, and van Gerkan + Marg in Germany; Benthem and Crouwel in Holland; Philippe Samyn in Belgium; Paul Andreu and Architecture Studio in France; Rafael Viñoly and Helmut Jahn in the United States; and Daryl Jackson and Philip Cox in Australia have all developed a similar style of architecture. In Japan,

during the fifties, the Metabolist movement proposed designs for urban growth involving the creation of megastructures, although these theories lost ground after the International Exhibition in Osaka in 1970. In spite of this, some of the architects involved in this movement such as Isozaki, Shinohara, and Kurokawa continue to show a particular interest in technological challenges.

Buildings of this type demand, in addition to the will and vision of the architect, continual advances in the technology of building materials. Research into the new possibilities of glass, steel, polycarbons, and aluminum has led to innovative formal solutions, in the same way that, at the beginning of the last century, the appearance of steel in architecture led to the construction of the Crystal Palace. In many ways, the companies who produce these new materials also promote their use and, consequently, provide an impulse for this new type of architecture. In short, technological development itself implies experimentation and use of the new materials.

Many of the firms producing these ground-breaking materials are closely associated with the aeronautical and aerospace industries, the construction of huge infrastructures such as oil rigs, underwater tunnels, or the new generation of suspension bridges. It is quite logical that there should be an osmosis between architecture and the scientific discoveries that are the driving force for these types of challenging structures. The introduction of powerful computer programs into the fields of architectural design and calculation is only the most recent example of this interplay between architecture and technology.

Architects such as Hiroshi Hara and Shin Takamatsu have exaggerated the technique until their designs come to resemble comics.

6,7. *Umeda Sky Building*
Osaka, 1993
Hiroshi Hara

8. *La Géode*
Paris, 1988
Adrien Fainsilber

9

In contrast to traditional construction techniques, the sophisticated tech-
nologies used today demand an extraordinary precision of detail. The use of
previously designed pieces means that the construction process becomes an
assembly line, similar to that of a car.

9. *El Palauet, Palafolls, 1996, Arata Isozaki*
10. *New Trade Fair, Leipzig, 1997, von Gerkan + Marg*

10

11, 12. *Norwandy bridge, Le Havre, 1995, Charles Lavigne*

17

The movement known as High-tech
has been mainly developed by British
architects such as Norman Foster,
Nicholas Grimshaw, Richard Rogers,
Ian Ritchie, etc.

13. *Law Faculty, Cambridge, 1995, Norman Foster*
14. *Hong Kong and Shanghai Bank, Hong Kong, 1986, Norman Foster*
15. *Bilbao Metro, Bilbao, 1995, Norman Foster*
16. *Business Promotion Center, Düsseldorf, 1994, Norman Foster*
17. *Commerzbank, Frankfurt, 1997, Norman Foster*

19

20

The attraction to the technical aesthetic has meant a parallel development in
industrial archaeology, dedicated to rescuing abandoned factories and warehouses
or to reproducing their decadent, rusted atmosphere.

Although the final look of their works may present certain similarities, the way in which Behnisch, Eisenman, and Moss approach their designs is completely different. Behnisch seeks the incorporation of new materials, integration with the environment, and absolute freedom of form, in designs without hierarchies or absolute models. The designs of Eisenman reproduce theoretic reflections which range from the inclusion of underlying historical traces to the development of spatial linguistics. Moss, in contrast, bases his research on geometrical experimentation.

1. *Hysolar Institute, Stuttgart, 1987, Günter Behnisch & Partner*

2. *Center for the Visual Arts, Ohio, 1988, Peter Eisenman*

3. *Lawson Westen House, Los Angeles, 1992, Eric Owen Moss*

After the Second World War, in contrast to the pristine clarity of the objectives of the Modern Movement, there was a succession of movements with diametrically opposed points of view, which gave rise to a tendency to generate complexity. While during the first half of the century, architects—like politicians, scientists, and intellectuals—tried to construct an ideal society of urban rationality, and more hygienic houses with light, in the latter half, the aim has been to "introduce noise into the system". In some ways, architectural developments since 1945 have either literally continued the premises established during the first half of the century or have been clearly opposed to them. From the fifties onward, the notion grew among some architects that the planned urbanism of former generations had been too mathematical and simplistic, and that, as such, it was insufficient to satisfy people's emotions.

The first explicit rupture took place during the IX CIAM congress in Aix-en-Provence, in 1953. The generation formed by the Smithsons, van Eyck, Candilis, and Bakema set up in opposition to the abstract vision of the city and began to study other forms of urban growth, following the structural theories beginning to emerge in anthropology, linguistics, and mathematics. In the seventies, the Archigram group, the Metabolists in Japan, and the International Situationists proposed a revision of architecture based on ideas which supported complex, random growth, which could not be previously designed in architectural studios. These theories were born of relativism and

accepted the mobility and continuous transformation of any initial design.

At the end of the seventies, a critique of the Modern Movement developed from a completely different perspective, also proposing greater heterogeneity. Firstly, Robert Venturi in his celebrated books *Complexity and Contradiction in Architecture* (1966) and *Learning from Las Vegas* (1972); later, Aldo Rossi with his defense of the typologies of the traditional city in *The Architecture of the City* (1966); finally, the kitsch and populist vision of Charles Jencks in *The Language of Postmodern Architecture* (1977). All of these writers try to recover forms of architecture that pre-date or are parallel to the Modern Movement and are closer to tradition and the popular aesthetic. These proposals materialized in postmodernism.

1

2

3

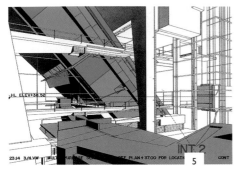

Graphic expression and the explanation
of the design have sometimes become
the final objective of the project, leaving
to one side the possible construction
of the design.

4. *Chemnitz Stadium, Chemnitz, 2002,
Peter Kulka*

5. *Design for the Tokyo International Forum,
1988, Neil Denari*

6. *Enlarged axonometric study
of the Victoria and Albert Museum,
London, 2003, Daniel Libeskind*

7. *Dub House, Holland, 1994, Bolles-Wilson*

8. *Research Center, Seibersdorf,
1995, Coop. Himmeb(l)au*

The ideas expressed in Kenneth Frampton's *Critical Regionalism* are halfway between the inheritance of modernism and its conceptual revision. In opposition to the populist trivialization of postmodernism, this prestigious architecture theorist proposed, at the end of the seventies and the beginning of the eighties, a recuperation of the rigor of the designs of the Modern Movement, but with the incorporation of the aesthetic of vernacular constructions in each region.

Another development occurred in 1988, when Philip Johnson, almost seventy years after organizing the exhibition Modern Architecture, was the guiding light behind another exhibition in the Museum of Modern Art of New York (MOMA), entitled Deconstructive Architecture. The title was obviously a reference to the theories of the French philosopher Jacques Derrida, but also to the Russian Constructivist movement of the first decades of the century. In fact, in his introduction to the exhibition catalogue, the associate director Mark Wigley accompanied his text with illustrations by Malevich, Tatlin, Rodchenko, and Chernikhov. The exhibition contained plans and working models by Frank. O. Gehry, Daniel Libeskind, Rem Koolhaas, Peter Eisenman, Zaha M. Hadid, Coop Himmelblau, and Bernard Tschumi. Philip Johnson himself commented that deconstructive architecture "is not a style. We cannot attribute to it even a modicum of the messianic fever of the Modern Movement. Deconstructive architecture does not represent a movement and it is not a creed. It does not have three obligatory rules".

As Johnson recognized, the architects represented in the exhibition had very differing points of view with respect to architecture and in no way they could be thought of as a group. In spite of this, deconstructivism spread rapidly, above all in the universities and architectural journals, with a success only comparable to the parallel repercussions it caused among the critical world—in art, literature, cinema, and even society in general. Undoubtedly, a large part of this success is due to the strong links that were established between architecture and text, and also to the importance given to publishing material—drawings and models—explaining constructed works. In fact, many of the protagonists of the exhibition were university lecturers who had produced many unconstructed designs which had a strong theoretical interest: both John Hedjuk and Peter Eisenman were associated with the Cooper Union of New York, while Rem

Koolhaas, Bernard Tschumi, Zaha Hadid, and Peter Wilson were all linked to the Architectural Association in London.

In the United States, the influence of deconstructivism was enormous, above all in the regions with a mild climate, such as California and Florida. Carlos Zapata, Asymptote, Mehrdad Yazdani, Josh Sweitzer, Eric Owen Moss, Michael Rotondi (ex-Morphosis), George Ranalli, Franklin D. Israel, Diller+Scofidio, Agrest & Gandelsonas, and Arquitectonica are some of the names which come to mind. This explosion should not be surprising if we remember that deconstructivism is full of spectacle, and many people would agree that few countries have such a well-developed sense of the spectacular as the United States. In Europe, although there are some isolated examples, the conceptual bases of deconstructivism soon became critically eroded and were substituted by new ideas and terminologies—nomad thinking, informalism, etc. In a way, whatever the name, what is known as deconstructivism is only one more facet of the succeeding ideas which have served to introduce congestion and complexity into architecture in the last fifty years.

Although we may no longer talk of deconstructivism, but instead use other terms, the majority of architects represented in Johnson's exhibition continue to design as many, or sometimes more, designs than in 1988. Frank Gehry, for example, has become a media phenomenon, with his works attracting as much attention as the latest Michael Jordan advert. The Guggenheim Museum in Bilbao is an exemplary case. The Basque Government freely admits the publicity gained is worth more than the cost of building the Museum—in other words, they got what they paid for. Buildings now transcend architecture and have become signs turned logotypes, postcards, or book covers. The same images which used to fill architectural journals now adorn tourist brochures. Libeskind is beginning to see his buildings actually built: the Jewish Museum in Berlin was finished in 1997 and the Victoria and Albert Museum will be inaugurated in the near future. From being a builder of dreams, in just a few years Eisenman has become a builder of buildings, although his constructions still retain their quality of great mental structures.

Zaha Hadid, Bernard Tschumi, and Coop Himmelblau—like other architects who did not participate in the exhibition, but have a similar presence in the same circles,

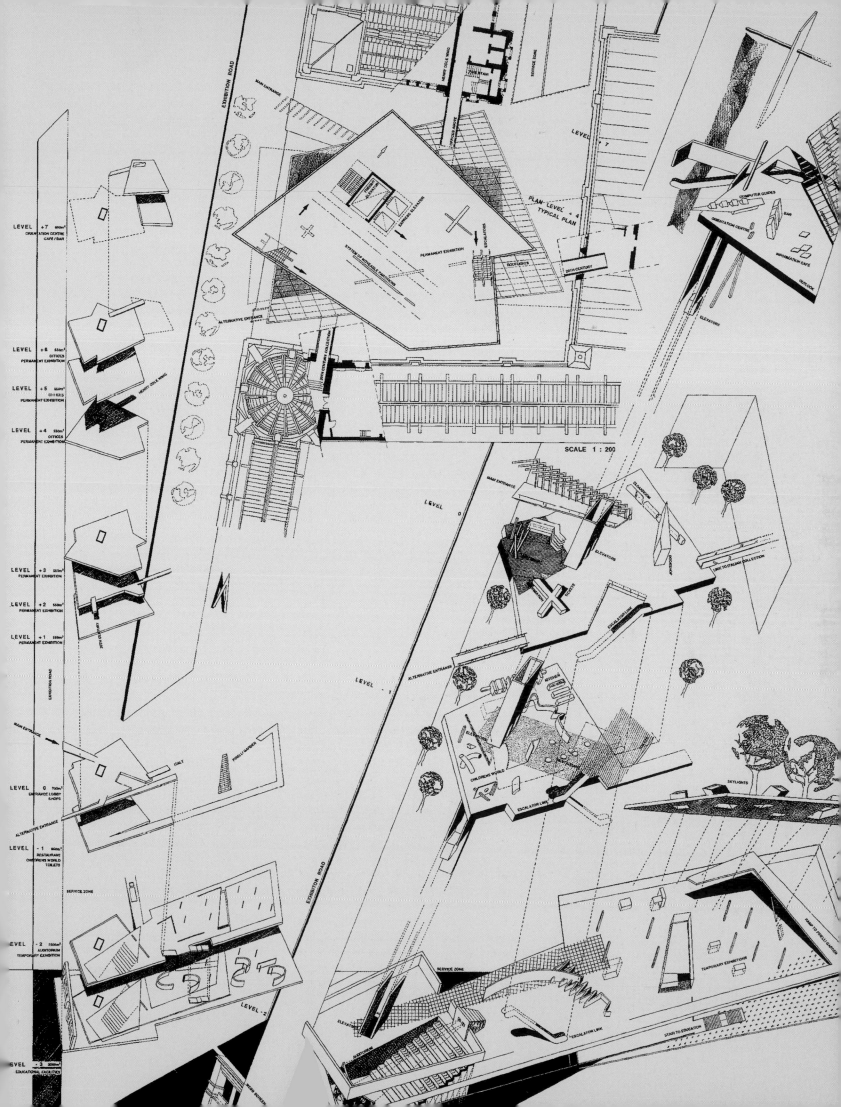

such as Morphosis, Enric Miralles or Bolles+Wilson—work in the same way as haute-couture designers. They construct few, but very costly buildings which require an enormous amount of resources. Their studios have become workshops where a large number of volunteer students participate—a type of test laboratory for formal experimentation.

The case of Rem Koolhaas is somewhat different: his designs are simultaneously a continuity and a negation of modern architecture. Koolhaas is a disbelieving and ironic modernist, whose influence has been extended by some of his direct disciples, such as Winy Maas (MVRDV), Adrian Geuze (West 8), and Stefano de Martino, and by many other young architects who share his theories, such as Mecanoo, Xaveer de Geyter, Stéphane Beel, Josep Lluís Mateo, Ben van Berkel, Yves Brunier, Florian Beigel, etc.

Mecanoo and Erick van Egeraat (a former member, now independent), are an interesting case; in some of their designs, they have proposed a strict revision of the models of the Modern Movement based on the use of the same typologies, but with current-day materials, finishes, and sensibilities.

9

One of the reasons for the quality and international success achieved by the architecture of a small country like Holland has been the incorporation of working techniques from fields such as graphic design, the plastic arts, and the world of photography and the image. The name of Rem Koolhaas has become an obligatory reference in current Dutch architecture for leading this revolution.

9. *Theater of Dance, The Hague, 1987, Rem Koolhaas*
10. *Kunsthal, Rotterdam, 1992, Rem Koolhaas*
11. *Design for Schouwburgplein, Rotterdam, 1995, West 8*
12. *Secondary school, Utrecht, 1997, Erick van Egeraat*
13. *WoZoCos, Amsterdam, 1997, MVRDV*
14. *Shopping Center, Emmen, 1996, Ben van Berkel*
15. *Housing in Haarlemmerbuurt, Amsterdam, 1995, Claus & Kaan*

10

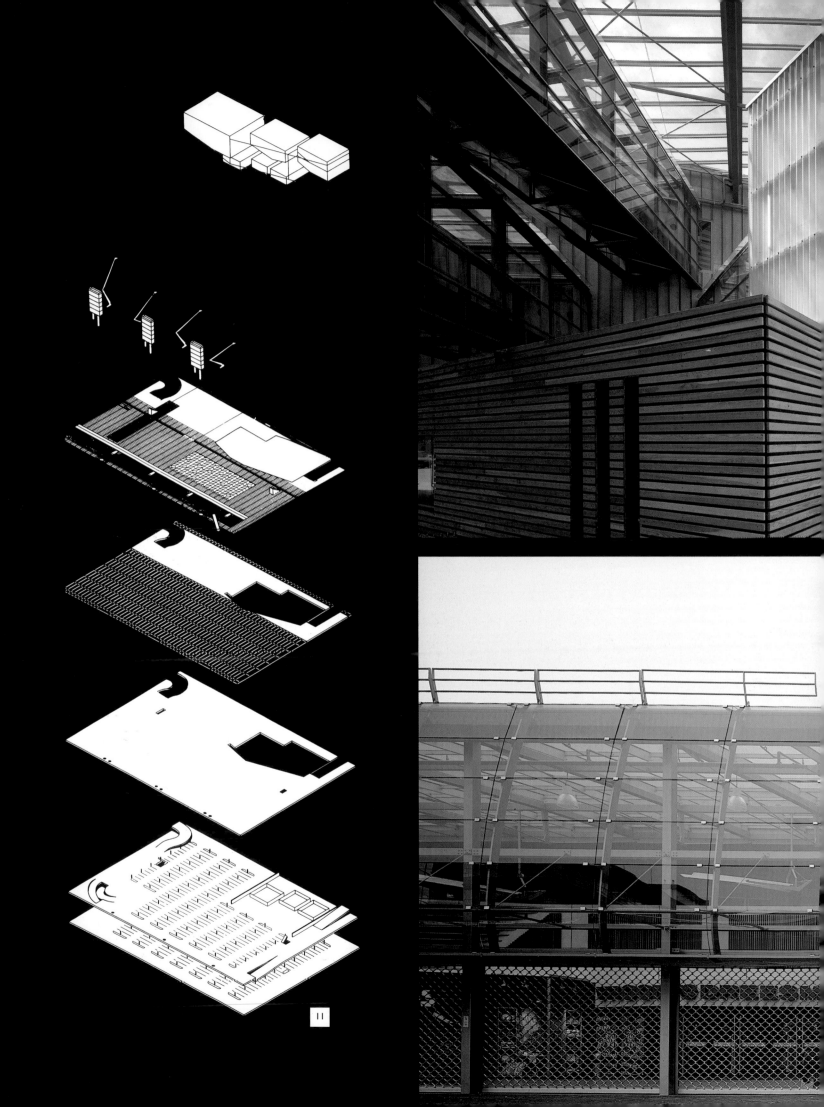

12

13

14

15

16

17

During the last decade, Frank O. Gehry's works have ceased to be compositions of slightly deformed, simple volumes such as cubes, pyramids, etc., and have been transformed into warped metal skins. This change has been made possible by the use of advanced computer programs.

16. *Guest pavilion of Winton Residence, Minnesota, 1987, Frank O. Gehry*

17. *Herman Miller furniture factory, Rocklin, California, 1987, Frank O. Gehry*

18. *Guggenheim Museum, Bilbao, 1997, Frank O. Gehry*

The agreeable climate and the large number of detached houses built have turned California into a paradise for those with original designs. There always seems to be someone ready to pay for something different.

19. *Blades House, Santa Barbara, 1997, Morphosis*

20. *House on Capistrano Beach, Capistrano Beach, California, 1994, Rob Wellington Quigley*

Two contiguous designs: while Eduard Bru juggles with urban elements, Miralles plays with topography.

21. *Urbanization of the Vall d'Hebron, Barcelona, 1992, Eduard Bru*

22. *Olympic Shooting Range, Barcelona, 1992, Enric Miralles*

Architecture for leisure

Leisure activities seem to be aimed at making up for the things that are lost or damaged during working hours—nature and our dreams.

1. *Elephant Jungle*
Seattle, Washington, 1991
Jones & Jones

2. *Nasu Highland Park*
Nasu, 1996
SWA Group

3. *Aquarium of Pont Defiance Zoo*
Tacoma, Washington, 1981
Jones & Jones

Nobody would deny that the leisure industry has become one of the driving forces of the world's economy in the last few decades. We only have to look at the film industry, the second biggest exporter in the United States, or the rock singers, sports stars, and television personalities who top the rankings every year, to say nothing of their astronomical earnings.

For some years now, entertainment, and the business it generates, has been a major economic factor. The construction of a huge theme park like Eurodisney generated a bitter struggle between the French and Spanish governments to convince the executives of the multinational company of the benefits of their respective countries. Tourism has become an increasingly important factor in the economies of many countries, and some regions such as the Balearic Islands, the Canary Islands, or Corfu live almost exclusively from other people's holidays. Hand-in-hand with this economic boom in tourism and leisure has come another factor: the increasing association of leisure with almost every type of individual product. If we accept the obvious—that in the developed world, we consume not to cover our needs but to satisfy our appetites—then we can see that the purchase of any product, from yogurt to sports shoes, tables to cars, is governed by

the pleasure factor. The decision to buy a yogurt rather than an apple, or indeed, not to eat at all, is governed largely by factors which have little to do with nourishment in its strictest sense. Logically, if people buy to satisfy a desire, marketing strategies will focus on encouraging those desires, and thus we have reached the situation where advertising and publicity campaigns are focused more on the ideas associated with the product than the product itself. We might say that the great challenge for salesmen and advertisers is to turn consumption into a leisure activity in itself, and in fact one of the most popular leisure activities people confess to is precisely "going shopping".

The economic importance of leisure in present-day society has led to an extraordinary development of the means designed for people to enjoy themselves. Every year, novel forms of "having a good time" appear, and new types of leisure center spring up. The possibilities for leisure and entertainment are much greater today than in any other epoch. As a reflection of this, architects have been faced with the need to design hitherto unknown types of building—indoor ski slopes, gigantic Imax cinemas, stadiums for exhibitions of windsurfing or motorcycle trials, etc.

One clear example of this trend is the great theme parks, a relatively recent innova-

1

2

3

4

tion, although its most obvious precursors are the zoos and aquariums which became popular in the second half of the last century. What is fundamental in a theme park is that visitors should be able to forget the daily problems which beset them—work, the education of their children, money, mortgages, etc.—and lose themselves in an entirely different environment which presents an unreal vision of life, full of imagination and fantasy.

The first park built by Disney in California, in 1956, was born with the avowed vocation of becoming "Dreamland". Most of the park was dedicated to the places and characters made famous in Disney's famous cartoon films. Other classic parks, such as Efteling, built in Holland in 1950, are based on other legendary characters: gnomes. Today there are themes for everyone—pirates, the conquest of space, the Middle Ages, Asterix and Obelix, the Circus, the Far West, even the Smurfs—all existing outside "real life". For the architect commissioned to build one of these centers, besides the usual factors such as the distribution of space, capacity, lighting, constructive system, and layout, it is perhaps equally, or more, important to be able to interpret the collective imagination of the visitor. The final "look" of the theme park should resemble a huge stage where visitors are invited to become the actors in their own fantasy. The job of the architect is to convert into three dimensions whatever comic book characters or cinema scenes are appropriate to the particular fantasy, while at the same time disguising services such as restaurants, ticket-booths, toilets, and shops with façades of enchanted castles or pirate ships.

Today, thematic architecture is by no means restricted to theme parks. Other types of building which house leisure activities, such as cinemas, restaurants, discotheques, and even shopping centers, are adopting an imaginative, appealing, and colorful aesthetic. The last few years have seen the seemingly unstoppable rise of thematic restaurants such as Planet Hollywood, the Hard Rock Café, and Dive!, where the actual food is only one small element of the visual spectacle offered. Once again, the architecture of leisure substitutes daily reality with an imaginary universe. Even the smallest traces of authenticity are eliminated. In this way, the nature of architecture is inverted, ceasing to be the construction of reality, to become rather the construction of unreality. The cri-

teria by which architecture is normally judged lose their meaning. The most important thing is that the building should be more attractive, more original and more fun than the competition.

Given this situation, if we assume (without being kill-joys) a parallel, autonomous aesthetic of construction, it becomes evident that the great dilemma is in determining where "thematic" architecture ends and "real" architecture begins. The American architect Robert Venturi suggests, in his book *Learning from Las Vegas*, that mainstream architecture should pay close attention to the great popularity of the capital of gambling and entertainment. Many postmodern buildings are in fact nothing more than thematic constructions whose defining shape aims to mimic an image from history. In the same way that a theme park recreates a pirate ship, the architect who designs a house to look like a Greek temple is attempting to satisfy the client's most avid fantasies, and not their daily, functional needs. What is more, not only the somewhat innocent caricatures of the postmodernists but also many of the most "revolutionary and formally risky" designs in architecture are nothing more than caricatures calculated for the media coverage they generate. The roll-call of architects contracted by Disney in recent years—Aldo Rossi, Frank Gehry, Arata Isozaki—speaks for itself.

Sport may be seen as an independent and separate category within the concept of leisure. Considered as an individual activity, designed for cultivation of the body and personal self-enrichment, sport is, in the Greek sense, culture. However, if we consider professional sport in its most multitudinous manifestations—football, the NBA, the Olympics—we are confronted with a spectacle whose participants are vastly outnumbered by the spectators. In spite of the vast difference between amateur, personal sport and the professional variety, the architecture in both cases is surprisingly honest. There are no tricks in a neighborhood gymnasium, nor in a football stadium. The importance of the event, of the match about to take place, concentrates the attention. Here, architecture is not obliged to distract, entertain, or even impress: the passion is on the pitch. This, combined with the very importance of the structure—the huge stands, the massive flying roofs—means that these stadiums are more akin to the honest vision of the engineer than that of architecture.

4. *Port Aventura, Salou, 1995,*
   Peckham, Guyton, Albers & Viets

5. *Florida Aquarium, Tampa, 1995,*
   Hellmuth, Obata & Kassabaum

6, 7, 8. *Nasu Highland Park*
       Nasu, 1996
       SWA Group

6

7

9

10

11

12

13

14

15

16

17

18

19, 20. Childhood has become the golden calf of our age. While young people reject maturity, adults try, at all costs, to recover their lost youth.

Public baths have been centers for leisure ever since the times of the Roman Empire.

21. *Sydney Aquatic Center, Sydney, 1994, Philip Cox*
22. *Itäkeskus Swimming Complex, Helsinki, 1993, Hyvämäki, Karhunen, Parkkinen*

24

23. *Bar of the Il Palazzo Hotel, Fukuoka, 1990, Shiro Kuramata*

23   24. *Gran Velvet discotheque, Barcelona, 1993, Alfredo Arribas*

Restaurants with a theme are becoming increasingly common.

25. *Caroline's Comedy Club, New York, 1993, Paul Haigh*
26. *Nobu, New York, 1994, David Rockwell*
27. *Zoë, New York, 1992, Jeffrey Beers*
28. *Americas, Houston, 1993, Jordan Mozer*
29. *Thèatron, Mexico City, 1996, Philippe Starck*

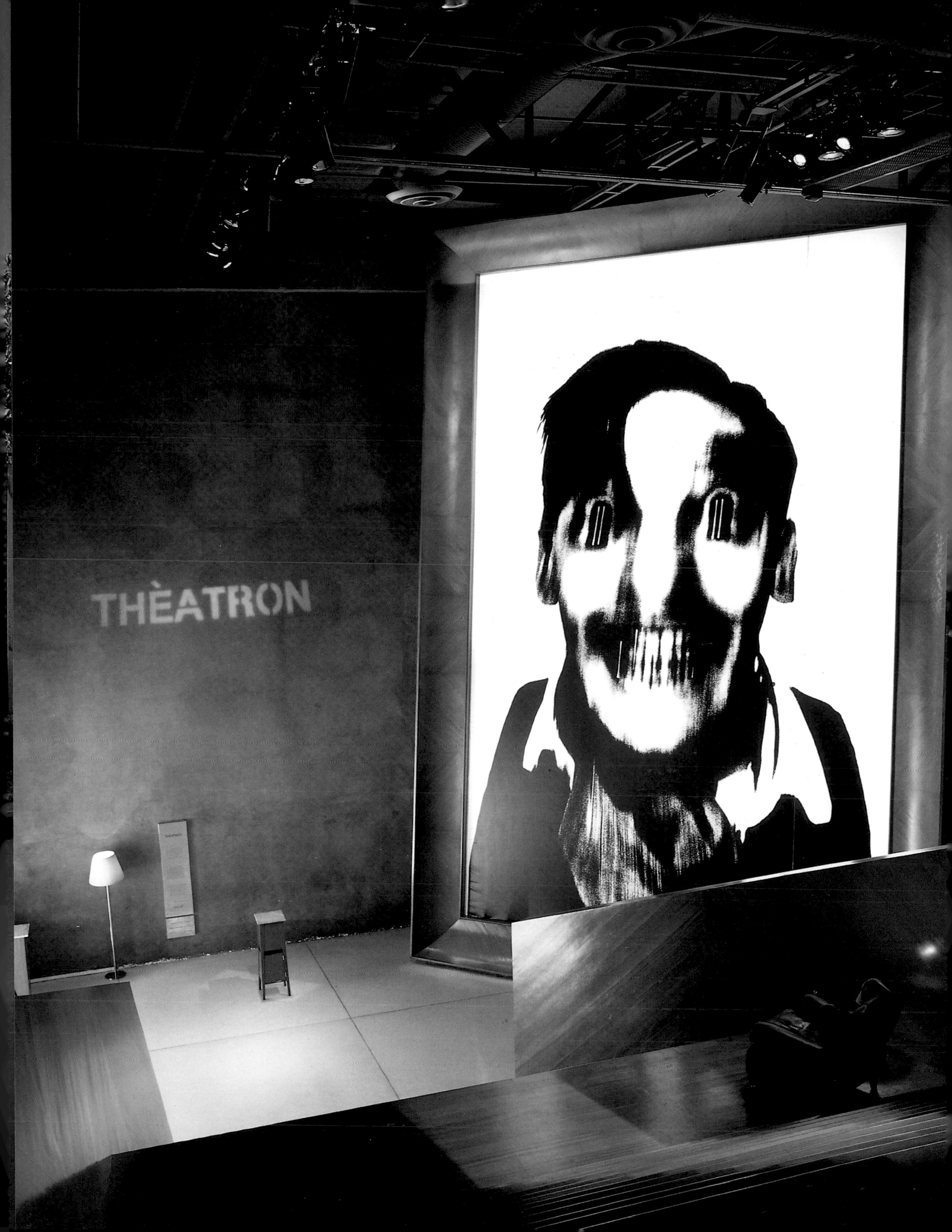
THÈATRON

houses are a reflection of habits, tastes, and personal preferences and can be seen as an exercise in self-knowledge on both sides.

While all this may be true for the individually designed house, the very opposite holds true for mass or collective housing, where the blocks or units are constructed with absolutely no thought for the individuals who will inhabit them. Collective housing has, perhaps, been the dominant theme in the architecture of this century. For the Modern Movement it was almost the only subject worth treating, as it was for the structuralists and situationists. However, as the end of the century approaches, it seems that architects have thrown in the towel and that the landscape is barren, judging from the lack of innovative designs of quality. Architectural journals contain few designs for blocks of apartments or condominiums, giving their space to museums, theatres, schools, skyscrapers, and, at most, individual, detached homes. Architects no longer passionately discuss the nature of collective housing and seem to have abandoned the subject to the mercies of the cost calculations of the developers and the mortgage interests of the banks.

Housing costs play a large part in nearly all family budgets. The house is where the intimate life of each individual is played out, the receptacle of individual illusions and hopes. And yet houses are produced en masse. Increasingly and, it must be said, with ever more explicitness and less dissimulation, blocks of apartments are built in conformance with a set of invariable prototypes. Bedrooms, kitchens, and bathrooms are built in accordance with the legal minimum requirements, without any individuality, as if the

residence were a product like brake fluid or soap powder.

The nature of each individual's needs and tastes with respect to their dwelling place, is, to say the least, an inexact science, but in spite of this, builders persist in repeating the same formulas almost with mathematical precision. Risk is avoided in the distribution of space, in the materials, the finishes, the typologies—in everything. If we consider how the family structure has radically changed over recent decades—in cities like New York or London, the one-person family unit is by far the most common—it would seem that to continue designing for the traditional couple with three children is anachronistic, if not downright ludicrous. However, both architects and builders continue to insist that this is the only possible destination for their creations. One might think that the financial and emotional effort that a house, apartment, or condo demands of its owner would lead builders and architects, to say nothing of legislators, to rethink some of their established ideas, but sadly, this is not the case. The construction of homes is completely conditioned by the profit margin. Their design seems to be dedicated to searching for the most profitable ways of stacking people on top of each other rather than looking for ways of developing a pleasant and comfortable environment for the individual occupant. This progressive deterioration is partially compensated by the progress of domestic technology: new and improved machines which relieve us of housework or furniture whose design is adaptable to the lamentably deficient spaces provided by the architect.

3,4. The type of space required by a given activity varies according to cultural precepts.

In these two pictures: bedroom in a Western apartment and a tatami room in a Japanese house.

While Schöener House in Mexico City is grouped around the patio, Zorn Residence in Chicago has a two-story-high interior space which fulfills the same function and gives protection from the extreme climate of Illinois.

5. *Schöener House, Mexico City, 1994, Grupo LBC*
6. *Zorn Residence, Chicago, 1995, Krueck & Sexton*

In designing the domestic space, identification with the place is essential, not only regarding integration of architecture and landscape but, above all, to respond to the emotional relationship that the owner–who chose this site over others–has with his property.

7. *House in Sag Pond, The Hamptons*
New York, 1992
Mario Gandelsonas & Diana Agrest

7

Evidently, the responsibility for this situation is shared. It would be unjust to point the finger only at developers and builders—as in any other business, the bottom line is sacred in present-day capitalist society—, or at the inertia of our governments, or indeed at the speculative nature of the housing market. Architects are responsible inasmuch as designs bear their stamp and construction is supervised by them. They are responsible for their complicity and servile adherence to the idea that those who pay the piper call the tune. Even those who occupy the house pay the price of their passivity and conformity with what they have been given.

Given this panorama, it is not surprising that many people look for an older house or apartment to occupy, which, although it may require more maintenance or adjustment, often suits their particular needs in a way that a modern mass-produced design cannot.

The rise of the spaces known as lofts, typically an old industrial or commercial premises with high ceilings and open spaces, points to a need for individual expression which, perhaps surprisingly, has been taken up by relatively few promoters, illustrating once again the lack of thought and imagination which dominates modern housing programs.

The majority of the small number of really interesting designs that are built are, in fact, social housing projects of one type or another, where the profit motive is relegated to a discreet second place. Therefore, it is a pleasure to be able to finish this somewhat depressing survey with a look at a pleasant exception to the rule: a private housing initiative built in Fukuoka at the end of the eighties. In one of those small parcels of land that the Japanese are slowly and painstakingly reclaiming from the sea, a whole neighborhood was constructed simultaneously, and,

under the direction of Arata Isozaki, some of the best international architects were invited to contribute with designs. Although the overall result was somewhat disappointing—the aim was a district with a homogenous look, while precisely the opposite effect was achieved—the American Steven Holl and the Dutchman Rem Koolhaas managed to construct what are, perhaps, the two best examples of collective housing seen in recent years. Happily, the two lie side by side.

8

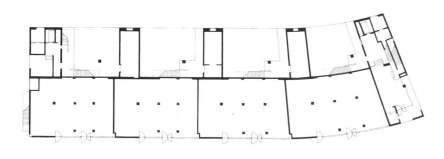

9. *General view of the residential complex. In the left foreground, the dwellings of Steven Holl, and to the right, those of Rem Koolhaas*

10,11. *Floor plans and interior views of Stephen Holl's dwellings in Fukuoka*

13

These two houses, designed by Campo Baeza and Nakao, accentuate the spiritual needs of the individual as opposed to the habitual pragmatism with which architects usually dissect the habits of their clients. The two projects seem to be the positive and negative sides of the same idea. While Gaspar House has patios inundated with light, Hiroshi Nakao has designed a space where the owner can sit and watch the rays of the sun cross the dark walls of his house throughout the day.

12. *Gaspar House, Cádiz, 1991, Alberto Campo Baeza*
13. *House for an ikebana artist, Tokorawa, 1996, Hiroshi Nakao*

Josep Juvé's house is full of objects and memories. Each detail is
conscientiously studied until total saturation of the space is achieved.
Hakuei House is just the opposite: the emptying of the space. While Western
culture is based on the accumulation of situations, Oriental society inclines
towards a space which is kept empty and may be used only occasionally.

14. *Architect's apartment, Barcelona, 1994, Josep Juvé*
15. *Hakuei House, Tokyo, 1996, Akira Sakamoto*

16

The best designs for collective housing in recent years have all been public initiatives. Sadly, the private sector has constructed projects in which the profit motive is unashamedly dominant.

16. *Kop van Zuid residential complex, Rotterdam, 1998, Frits van Dongen*
17. *Social housing in Alcobendas, Madrid, 1996, Manuel de las Casas*
18. *WoZoCos, Amsterdam, 1997, MVRDV*

17

18

20

21

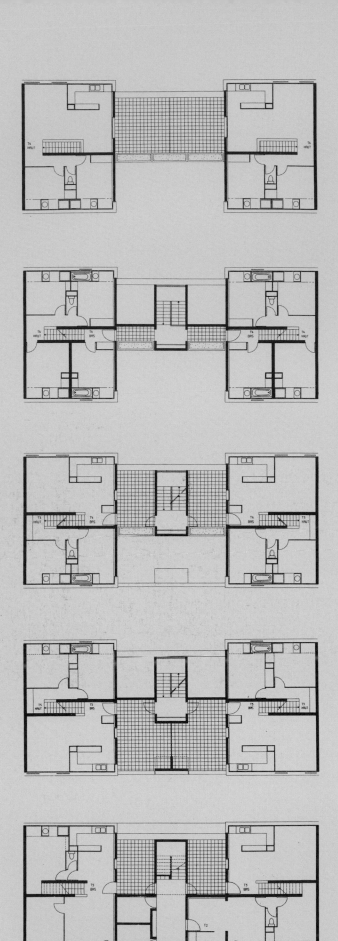

19

22

The most interesting designs of the French architect Yves Lion are all in the field of housing. Lion has proposed new ideas, such as placing the services in the façade of the building, and has rescued essential spaces such as the double-story terrace patio as originally suggested by Le Corbusier.

19, 20. *Housing in Villejuif*
Paris, 1994
Yves Lion

21. *Design for the Domus Demain*
competition, 1994

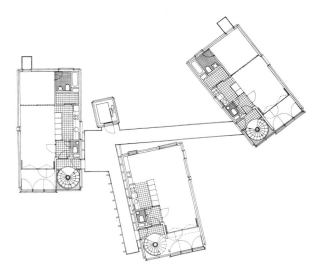

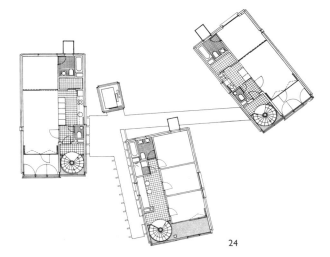

22, 23. Frits van Dongen has also succeeded in bringing the typology of "a house around a patio" to collective housing in his residential project, Kop van Zuid, Rotterdam, 1998.

Mecanoo separate the dwellings in such a way that although they form part of a collective block, sharing stairs and elevators, each apartment is surrounded by exterior space and has the atmosphere of an isolated house.

24. *Duplex, Stuttgart, 1991, Mecanoo*

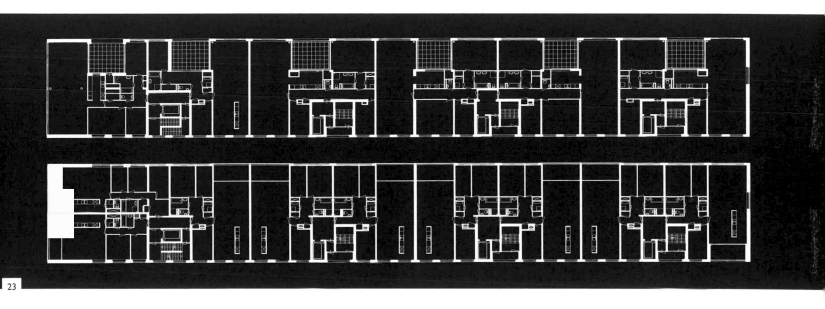

25, 26. The dwellings in Basle by Herzog & de Meuron also revolve around a community patio–a semiprivate space.

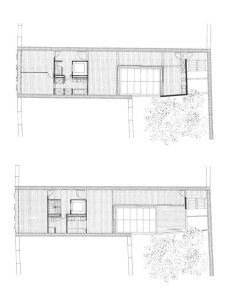

27

One of the great challenges of collective housing is
enabling the inhabitants to enjoy life in the open air.

27. *Penthouse apartment of a residential block,
Oporto, 1995, Eduardo Souto de Moura*
28. *Apartments for postal workers, Paris, 1993,
Philippe Gazeau*

Photographic credits

The heart of the city

Photo 1: Lawrence Raskin. Photo 2: Peter Aaron/Esto Photographics. Photo 3: Alessandro Gui. Photo 4: Kokyu Miwa. Photo 5: O.H. Fency. Photo 6: Gérard Dufresne. Photo 7: Georges Fessy. Photo 8: Magherita Spiluttini. Photo 9: David Cardelús. Photo 10: Luis Ferreira Alves. Photo 11: Hervé Abbadie. Photo 12: Hervé Abbadie. Photo 13: S.I. Andersson. Photo 14: Accent Visuel. Photo 15: Alan Ward. Photo 16: O.H. Fency. Photo 17: Cesar San Millán. Photo 19: Philippe Ruault. Photo 25: Jen Fong. Photo 26: Rocco Design Limited. Photo 27: Philippe Ruault. Photo 28: David Cardelús. Photo 30: Lourdes Legorreta. Photo 32: Osamu Murai.

Macrobuildings-Microcities

Photo 1: *Tomio Ohashi*. Photo 2: *Jannes Linders*. Photo 3: *Claes de Vrieselaan*. Photo 6: *Philippe Ruault*. Photo 7: *Accent Visuel*. Photo 9: *Nacása & Parthers*. Photo 10: *Paul Maurer*. Photo 11: *Kouji Okamoto*. Photo 12: *Accent Visuel*. Photo 13: *Paul Maurer*. Photo 14: *Paul Maurer*. Photo 17: *Philippe Ruault*. Photo 19: *Philippe Ruault*. Photo 20: *Kokyu Miwa*. Photo 21: *Ramon Camprubí*. Photo 22: *Ramon Camprubí*. Photo 23: *Klaus Frahm*. Photo 24: *Klaus Frahm*. Photo 25: *Paul Maurer*. Photo 26: *Philippe Ruault*.

The periphery

Photo 2: *Nobuaki Nakagawa*. Photo 3: *Eric Saillet*. Photo 5: *Peter Durant*. Photo 6: *Nacása & Parthers*. Photo 7: *Sylvie Bersout*. Photo 8: *David Cardelús* Photo 9: *Luis Gordoa*. Photo 10: *Stijn Brakkee*. Photo 11: *Sigurgeir Sigurjónsson*. Photo 12: *Sigurgeir Sigurjónsson*. Photo 13: *Sigurgeir Sigurjónsson*. Photo 14: *Nacása & Parthers* . Photo 15: *Nacása & Parthers*. Photo 16: *Gary Kuight & Associates*. Photo 17: *Gary Kuight & Associates*. Photo 18: *Pietro Savorelli*. Photo 19: *Sylvie Bersout*. Photo 20: *Kevin Conger*. Photo 21: *Manos Meisen*. Photo 22: *Margherita Spiluttini*. Photo 23: *Philippe Ruault*. Photo 24: *Bill Timmerman*. Photo 25: *David Cardelús*. Photo 27: *Margherita Spiluttini*. Photo 28: *Michael Denancé*. Photo 29: *Christian Richters*.

Topography and context

Photo sin numero: *Bjarne Aasen*. Photo 1: *David Cardelús*. Photo 2: *Jean-Michel Landecy*. Photo 3: *Satoshi Asakawa*. Photo 4: *Pablo Mason*. Photo 5: *Friederich Busam*. Photo 6: *Bard Ginnes*. Photo 8: *Ralph Richter*. Photo 9: *Nacása et Partners*. Photo 10: *Nacása & Partners* Photo 11: *Nacása & Partners*. Photo 12: *R. Maack*. Photo 13: *Bill Timmerman*. Photo 14: *Alfonso Cano*. Photo 15: *David Closas*. Photo 16: *Jussi Tiainen*. Photo 17: *Koumei Tanaka*. Photo 18: Jeroen Musch. Photo 19: Jeroen Musch. Photo 20: Jeroen Musch. Photo 21: Jeroen Musch. Photo 22: Jeroen Musch. Photo 23: Jeroen Musch. Photo 24: Jeroen Musch. Photo 25: *Dirk Reinartz*. Photo 26: *Werner Hannappel*.

Strategy and Metaphor

Photo 1: *David Cardelús*. Photo 3: *Lourdes Jansana*. Photo 5: *Ralph Richter*. Photo 6: *Ralph Richter*. Photo 7: *Ralph Richter*. Photo 9: *Timothy Hursley* Photo 10: *Richard Bryant*. Photo 11: *Richard Bryant*. Photo 12: *Richard Bryant*. Photo 13: *Richard Bryant*. Photo 14: *George Fessy*. Photo 15: *Paul Maurer* Photo 17: *Christian Kandzia*. Photo 18: *Christian Kandzia*. Photo 19: *Christian Kandzia*. Photo 20: *Christian Kandzia*. Photo 21: *David Cardelús*. Photo 22: *David Cardelús*. Photo 23: *David Cardelús*. Photo 24: *Yoshio Takase*. Photo 26: *Eugeni Pons*. Photo 27: Hisao Suzuki. Photo 28: Hisao Suzuki Photo 29: T. R. Darneb. Photo 31: T. R. Darneb. Photo 33: T. R. Darneb. Photo 34: T. R. Darneb. Photo 35: T. R. Darneb. Photo 36: A. Ward. Photo 37: J. Venezia. Photo 38: Philippe Ruault.

The persistence of the monument

Photo 1: *O. Mandrelli*. Photo 2: *Peter Cook*. Photo 4: *D ani Karavan*. Photo 5: *Tim Hursley*. Photo 6: *Georges Fessy*. Photo 7: *Georges Fessy*. Photo 8: *Robert Canfield*. Photo 9: *Lourdes Legorreta*. Photo 10: *Tim Hursley*. Photo 11: *Shigeo Ogawa*. Photo 12: *Eugeni Pons*. Photo 13: *Nacása & Partners*. Photo 14: *Fernando Alda*. Photo 15: *Octavi Mestre*. Photo 17: *S. Wewerka*. Photo 18: Nacása & Partners. Photo 19: *Andy Goldsworthy* Photo 20: *David Cardelús*. Photo 21: *Steve Martino*. Photo 22: Daniel Díaz Font. Photo 23: Tomio Ohashi. Photo 24: J. Apicella . Photo 25: *Koji Okamoto* Photo 26: *Murpy / Jahn*. Photo 27: *James H. Morris*. Photo 28: *José Moscardi Junior*.

Transparency and Opacity

Photo 1: *Michael Reisch*. Photo 2: *Kim Zwartz*. Photo 3: *Christian Richters*. Photo 4: *Futsitsuka Mitsumasa*. Photo 5: *Futsitsuka Mitsumasa*. Photo 6: *Futsitsuka Mitsumasa*. Photo 7: *Architekturphoto*. Photo 8: *Hervé Abbadie*. Photo 9: *Jussi Tiainen*. Photo 10: *Jussi Tiainen*. Photo 11: *Toshiharu Kitasima*. Photo 12: *Eduard Hueber*. Photo 13: *Christian Richters*. Photo 14: *Christian Richters*. Photo 15: *Tomio Ohashi*. Photo 18: *Margherita Spiluttini* Photo 19: *Christian Richters*. Photo 21: *Margherita Spiluttini*. Photo 22: *Ralph Richters*. Photo 23: *Philippe Ruault*.

The logic of the structure

Photo 1: *Sthéphane Couturier*. Photo 2: *J. M. Monthiers*. Photo 3: *Toshiharu Kitajima*. Photo 4: *F. Busam/Architekturphoto*. Photo 5: *F. Busam / Architekturphoto* Photo 6: *Tomio Ohashi*. Photo 7: *Tomio Ohashi*. Photo 9: *Eugeni Pons*. Photo 10: *F. Busam/Architekturphoto*. Photo 11: *S. Soane/Architekturphoto*. Photo 12: *S. Soane/Architekturphoto*. Photo 13: *Herman H. Van Doorn*. Photo 14: *Octavi Mestre*. Photo 15: *Lluís Sans*. Photo 17: *Richard Davies*. Photo 18: *Jo Reid*. Photo 19: *Jhon Peck*. Photo 20: *Eugeni Pons*. Photo 21: *Latz & Partner*.

Techniques of congestion

Photo 1: *Christian Kandzia*. Photo 3: *Tom Bonner*. Photo 7: *Christian Richters*. Photo 8: *Gerald Zugmann*. Photo 10: *Lock Images*. Photo 12: *Christian Richters*. Photo 13: *Hans Wercemann*. Photo 14: *Christian Richters*. Photo 15: *Ger van der Vlugt*. Photo 16: *Mark Darley*. Photo 17: *Nick Merrick* Photo 18: *Eugeni Pons*. Photo 19: *Kim Zwarts*. Photo 20: *Undine Prohl*. Photo 21: *David Cardelús*. Photo 22: *David Cardelús*.

Architecture for leisure

Photo 1: *Eduardo Calderón*. Photo 2: *Tom Fox*. Photo 4: *David Cardelús*. Photo 5: *Georgé Coft*. Photo 6: *Tom Fox*. Photo 7: *Tom Fox*. Photo 8: *Tom Fox* Photo 9: *David Cardelús*. Photo 10: *David Cardelús*. Photo 11: *David Cardelús*. Photo 12: *Druscilla Wiliams*. Photo 13: *Druscilla Wiliams*. Photo 14: *Tom Fox*. Photo 15: *Tom Fox*. Photo 16: *Fujitsuka Mitsumasa*. Photo 17: *Tom Fox*. Photo 18: *Tom Fox*. Photo 19: *Koo Basi*. Photo 20: *Fujitsuka Mitsumasa*. Photo 22: *Jussi Tiainen*. Photo 24: *David Cardelús*. Photo 25: *Elliot Kaufman*. Photo 26: *Paul Warchol*. Photo 27: *Paul Warchol*. Photo 29: *Dito Jacob*.

Domestic space

Photo 1: *Lluís Casals*. Photo 2: *Peter Hyatt*. Photo 3: *Eugeni Pons*. Photo 4: *Kaumei Tanaka*. Photo 5: *Fernando Cordero*. Photo 6: *Korad Hedrich Blessing* Photo 7: *Paul Warchol*. Photo 9: *Richard Barnes*. Photo 10: *Richard Barnes*. Photo 11: *Richard Barnes*. Photo 12: *Nacása & Partners*. Photo 13: *Hisao Suzuki*. Photo 14: *Eugeni Pons*. Photo 15: *Nacása & Partners*. Photo 16: *Daria Scagliola*. Photo 17: *Eduardo Sánchez*. Photo 18: *Hans Werlemann* Photo 22: *Daria Scagliola*. Photo 25: *Margherita Spiluttini*. Photo 26: *Luiz Ferreira Alves*. Photo 27: *Jean Marie Monthiers*.